"Would it really make a d
time alone with God eve
your life has anything to d̲ ̲.̲.̲.̲.̲.̲.̲ ̲s̲e̲e̲i̲n̲g̲ a revival take place
in your city, nation, or your family? Well I guess there's only
one way to find out... start doing it! Kari's daily reflec-
tions on her own journey with God would be a great way to
begin. I'm sure you will find your own personal journey an
exciting one. Fasten your seat belts and begin today!"

—Rev. Larry G. Jahnke
Founding Pastor, New Song Church
Bismarck, ND

"This devotional book is an outflow of Kari's love for the
Word of God and her commitment to prayer. It will challenge the reader with insightful thoughts and give directives in the area of prayer. As believers, if we are going
to become strong spiritually and have an impact on our
communities, we must develop an appetite for the Word
and a consistent prayer life. This book will assist you in
developing that discipline."

—Rev. Leon D. Freitag,
N.D. District Superintendent

"Kari Bitz brings the emphasis of her life to this book.
Her steadfast seeking of God through prayer and fasting
is shown throughout this devotional. I really like the wide,
vast variety of subjects dealt with on a daily basis. The daily
request section is so powerful and creative in teaching us
how to pray. I whole heartedly recommend the use of this
book as a tool of hearing and communicating with God."

—Pastor Roger L. Will
Evangel, Bismarck, ND

PEOPLE-CENTERED
prayer

KARI BITZ

PEOPLE-CENTERED
prayer

A Daily Devotional

for Ourselves, Our Friends,

and Our Leaders

TATE PUBLISHING
AND ENTERPRISES, LLC

Published by Tate Publishing & Enterprises, LLC
127 E. Trade Center Terrace | Mustang, Oklahoma 73064 USA
1.888.361.9473 | www.tatepublishing.com

Tate Publishing is committed to excellence in the publishing industry. The company reflects the philosophy established by the founders, based on Psalm 68:11,
"The Lord gave the word and great was the company of those who published it."

Book design copyright © 2012 by Tate Publishing, LLC. All rights reserved.
Cover design by Joel Uber
Interior design by Nathan Harmony

Published in the United States of America

ISBN: 978-1-61862-833-6
1. Religion / Christian Life / Devotional
2. Religion / Christian Life / General
12.03.22

Dedication

This book is dedicated to the many churches
from many denominations that united together
to kick off a 40 week focus in prayer and fasting

and to my dear husband.

Contents

Introduction

When I was young, I would take a sack lunch to my favorite place on the lower end of a mountain where there was a rock cut with beautiful colorations. I would go there alone to spend time with God. It was a getaway and my rest for the day. It is in the presence of God that we find rest for our souls and from the busyness of the day.

Years later, after marrying and having children, I began to sense God's call in my life. My family uprooted itself and moved to a state with mountains. We had always enjoyed the vacations there and thought we would enjoy the activities that we could do there. But even before this began the most difficult year of my life—a release of everything in my life to God. God broke me during those months. I was challenged in every area of my life to lay down my hopes and dreams. I prayed and asked God what was happening and all that came to mind was "testing." I went through a period of testing that placed in my soul a vision of national revival to come, seared through fiery trials. I am reminded of Genesis 47:31. "And Israel worshiped leaning on the top of his staff." He was never the same after wrestling with God.

Through this severe time for me, a vision came alive in my soul, and has not been able to die. It was seared through the most fiery of trials. It was a vision of great revival to come in the wake of unprecedented prayer and fasting which tends to be how revivals have come in the past.

To this end I write, allowing God to guide me. As the story of the servants with the talents, God requires us to use what we have been given for His service. He does not expect us to be perfect but rather to use the gifts and talents that He gives. And the greatest fulfillment in our lives will surely be in obeying God. Each one of us has a call of God in our lives to follow Him. He has a specific plan for our lives, and He desires that we find rest for our souls in Him. It is most surely in the presence of God that we find our greatest fulfillment and growth.

My desire in writing this book is that you will be drawn to a closer relationship with God and filled with His blessings and favor. As we draw closer to God, He is able to fill us with truth, love, and His Spirit in increasing measure. My personal vision in life is a call to see national repentance—a nation changed by the power of God through united prayer and even fasting. Acts 3:19 says, "Repent and turn to God, so that your sins may be wiped out, that times of refreshing may come." It is through turning to God and making Him our Lord that times of refreshing come in our lives and in our nation. We follow God to pray for our nation, our communities, and our own lives.

I believe we are missing out on one of the calls of God for us to make a difference in our lifetime partly due to priorities and also due to the business of life. We must make the time to reach out, to pray and to make God our first priority in love. Then the other things will fall into place. If we get the building blocks in place, the extras line themselves up more easily.

So many times I talk to people who do not know what to pray for our regions, communities and even nation. They become bored with the usual and tire of praying. But prayer is the way that God has ordained to make great difference in our nation, communities, and own lives. Prayer is the starting point, a building block that we need. *"Ask and you will receive and your joy will be complete (John 16:24)."* One of the key ingredients in our Christian walk that we are missing out on is joy, which here, is promised from prayer. This devotional includes requests to ask God for our own lives, our communities, and for the nation. If you would like to apply it to your loved ones and family, pray it for them as well. Just apply the first request to your life and your family as well.

Many times people do not know how to pray a request. They look at it and wonder how to pray it. So this devotional has one of the prayer requests written out, simply, at the bottom of each devotional. This will give you examples that you can use daily for praying the requests. May God bless you as you begin to establish a prayer life that will make a difference for generations to come.

One more thought for the road is this. As a youth I made a commitment to read the Bible every day because God says that His Word will not return without an effect. It will make a difference (Isaiah 55:11, NKJV). There were times I inevitably woke up late and had less time to read but I applied the principle of reading at least a verse a day.

So I have put a verse a day in each devotional. If you do not get the entire devotional read, read at least the verse and come back to it later. The habit that you begin will pay off for years to come.

I am here because of God's call to see revival come to a nation. What is revival? It is to revive the heart and soul and spirit of people. It is to impassion people.

When life's trials are difficult and the world around us is in uproar, we need God's presence to bring peace and rest to our souls. I have learned to come to the cross and find revival and refreshing in the One who paid it all.

Jesus said, "Come to me, all you who are weary and burdened, and I will give you rest" (Matthew 11:28).

Wherever You Go

> "Have I not commanded you? Be strong and courageous. Do not be terrified; do not be discouraged, for the Lord your God will be with you wherever you go" (Joshua 1:9).

God commanded Joshua to be strong and courageous. It wasn't a recommendation or an idea, but rather a command. God called Joshua to lead and required him to be strong and courageous to do it. On the outside, decisions and steps of faith may look terrifying, but when we look from God's view, we can see that we are able to do what He calls us to do, even when we fear it.

How comforting it is to know that God is with you wherever you go. He says, "I will never leave you nor forsake you" (Hebrews 13:5). That is why we can be courageous in the midst of difficulties or threats.

Do you know that God is with you wherever you go?

Do we ever lose our faith in being able to accomplish what we have to do? God told Joshua here to be strong and courageous. He was to lead the Israelites into the promised land. He told him to not be fearful or discouraged because He would be with Him wherever he went. God was standing by His side to give Him success.

Is there something that God is calling you to do? Be obedient. Fear not. It is God who enables.

Daily Requests

- Pray that we will sense God's presence and not fear.

- Ask God to draw people to love Him and to love others.

- Pray for national repentance.

Lord, we ask that you bring people in the nation to repentance. We pray that Your Spirit will bring conviction of sin in the nation.

Mercy not Sacrifice

"As Jesus went on from there, he saw a man named Matthew sitting at the tax collector's booth. 'Follow me,' he told him, and Matthew got up and followed him. While Jesus was having dinner at Matthew's house, many tax collectors and 'sinners' came and ate with him and his disciples. When the Pharisees saw this, they asked his disciples, 'Why does your teacher eat with tax collectors and "sinners?"' On hearing this, Jesus said, 'It is not the healthy who need a doctor, but the sick... But go and learn what this means: "I desire mercy, not sacrifice""' (Matthew 9:9-13).

Jesus didn't always do what looked right to the Pharisees (religious leaders) and other people. He cared about sinners. He had mercy on them. He spent time with them even though He looked wrong to some. They were not the respectable people in their society or culture.

God came to draw sinners to repentance. He wants us to show mercy to others more than sacrifice to him. Sacrifice involves giving up something. Mercy is a genuine love and compassion on those who need help or are hurting. It is to reach out to others as Jesus would.

Jesus rebuked the Pharisees who did all the "right" sacrifices. They followed the laws and regulations but did not have love or mercy on others. We are to follow Christ and love those who are hurting and those who are living in sin. Jesus did the same for us. He died for us while we were yet sinners. Pray for people around you. Reach out to them. Get to know them. Care about them. Jesus did.

Daily Requests

- Pray for God to reveal Himself in mighty ways in our family and relationships.

- Ask God to draw us to Himself and give us His heart for those around us.

- Pray that God will pour out His Spirit upon the nation and give people a felt need for Christ.

Lord, we ask that You would reveal Yourself to us, and give us love for those around us.

Fret Not at All

"Therefore do not worry about tomorrow, for tomorrow will worry about itself. Each day has enough trouble of its own" (Matthew 6:34).

Before this verse, Jesus tells us to make the Kingdom of God your primary concern. In other words, seek first the kingdom of God (the things of God). Place your focus and eyes on Him rather than the possessions of the world and what you will eat or drink. Do not concern yourself with money primarily but rather with doing God's will and obeying Him. Serve the Lord and obey Him. Trust Him. There are blessings with obedience.

We do not know what tomorrow will bring, but we know that the Father in heaven promises to take care of us. When we place Him first, He will take care of tomorrow's concerns. Is it easy not to worry about tomorrow? What is it that concerns you the most? Take it to God. Make Him your primary focus and trust Him to take care of tomorrow's concerns. Look back at God's faithfulness in the past.

Remember the goodness of God and how He supplies your needs. Share it with others. Allow your testimony to shine into other people's lives. Remember, seeds can be sown through your testimony that God can use for years to come.

Daily Requests

- Ask for opportunities to share your testimony with others.

- Pray for the goodness of God to well up in the body of Christ.

- Ask God to raise up workers and harvesters in the nation for His glory.

Lord, we ask for open doors to share with those around us and help us be a witness to them. Give us ideas and eyes that see the open doors.

Turn from Evil

> "He must turn from evil and do good; he must seek peace and pursue it. For the eyes of the Lord are on the righteous and His ears are attentive to their prayer, but the face of the Lord is against those who do evil" (1 Peter 3:10-12).

What is righteousness? It is to be in right standing with God. We are made righteous by faith in Christ. Our faith reveals itself by being active. We are to turn away from evil and do good. When evil or temptation presents itself, we are to turn around and face the opposite direction.

Joseph, when tempted by his master's wife, turned around and ran in the opposite direction. He even left his jacket behind. He was wrongly accused because of it, and he ended up in prison. But the Lord saw, knew he was innocent, brought him out of prison, and blessed him. Joseph ended up with God's blessings. Before God, he was righteous. God knew he had done the right thing and resisted temptation (Genesis 39).

Time and again throughout history, we see accounts of God's goodness and mercy in the lives of those who are obedient to Him regardless of other's accusations. We also see that God answers the prayers of the righteous. He is attentive to our prayers. He turns His ear to us to hear what we are asking of Him.

Daily Requests

- Pray for God's people to line up with His Word and trust Him.

- Ask God to guide and direct us into His will.

- Ask God to soften the hearts of people in the nation to Him.

Father in heaven, we ask that we will be convicted to turn from evil and do good and to seek peace and pursue it.

Seek Good

"Seek good, not evil, that you may live. Then the Lord God Almighty will be with you, just as you say He is. Hate evil, love good; maintain justice in the courts" (Amos 5:14-15a).

Life comes from God. If you desire to abide in life, you must seek good and not evil. You must pursue good. Actively seek it. Then the Lord will be with you, and you will have His blessings. It actually says that "you will live" when you seek good and not evil. The result is life that is rich and abundant, and He who created the ends of the earth will be on your side.

Love must be sincere. Love what is good. Hate what is evil (Romans 12:9).

Life is good. Love life. Love what is good. Then you will be an example to others of God's grace. Others will be drawn to God's goodness and to His side. If we will set an example for others in our life with what we support and love, people will be drawn to Christ. They will be drawn to truth. We are to be the salt and light. We are to turn ourselves toward good and away from evil.

Do not support sin. When others are sinning around you, do not laugh with it. Do not engage in it or mimic it. If possible, find a way to draw others to what is good instead. Change the subject. Avoid evil. And decide to serve God even when others don't.

Daily Requests

- Pray that we will know and discern good from evil.

- Ask God to convict His family (Christians) of righteousness.

- Pray for godly leaders to make an impact in the nation for God's glory.

Lord God, we ask that You will raise up godly leaders who will listen to Your leading and follow it and make a mighty impact for Your glory and honor.

PEOPLE-CENTERED PRAYER   31

Love Your Enemies

> "But I say to you, love your enemies, bless those who curse you, do good to those who hate you, and pray for those who spitefully use you and persecute you" (Matthew 5:44).

A way to be an example of Christ's love is to treat others in an opposite manner of what the world expects. When they have hurt you—love them instead.

If people persecute you for being a Christian or look down on you for it, then pray for them and act in a loving way with patience and kindness. It will sow seeds into their lives of Christian testimony that God is different. If we want people to come to Christ, we must act differently from the world.

What do we do different from those that persecute us? To spitefully use someone is to have a malicious, damaging intent. It is a willful plan to harm someone. We must not succumb to bitterness. Pray for your enemies.

Daily Requests

- Ask God to give us His heart for the lost.

- Pray for opportunities to shine Christ to others and give us His love for them.

- Pray for people in the nation to love God and decidedly make the commitment to follow Him.

Lord God, we need You. We ask You to open doors of opportunity to shine Christ to those around us, and we ask that You give us Your love for them.

What God Has Prepared

> "However, as it is written: 'No eye has seen, no ear has heard, no mind has conceived what God has prepared for those who love him'" (1 Corinthians 2:9, 13).

As the children of God and as those who love Him, God has prepared such things for us that are beyond what we can understand as humans. Our minds are finite and limited without the Holy Spirit's help. We need His enablement to know what He has prepared for us.

What human mind would have conceived the plan of God that brought salvation to us? To send His only begotten Son to live among us and to fulfill thousands of prophecies in the Old Testament was the plan of God not man. He revealed Himself to us through His Son's life, death, and resurrection. It was a plan that our finite minds cannot understand without the help of the Holy Spirit.

Ask God to reveal what He has planned for you. Ask Him for illumination and understanding. If you want to know something, ask God to reveal it to you.

This is what we speak, not in words taught us by human wisdom, but in words taught by the Spirit, expressing spiritual truths in spiritual words (verse 13). Only with God can we understand the good things He has for us.

Daily Requests

- Ask God to anoint us with His Spirit to understand the things of God.

- Pray for the lost to come to an understanding of the greatness of God's love for them.

- Ask God to bring revival and awakening in the nation.

Jehovah Jireh, we pray for the unsaved to come to an understanding of the depth, the width, the length, and the height of Your love for them.

The Word became Flesh

> "The Word became flesh and made his dwelling among us. We have seen His glory, the glory of the one and only Son, who came from the Father, full of grace and truth" (John 1:14).

God sent His Son in human form to dwell among us. God sent His love upon us by sending His one and only Son, Jesus, that we might have access to Him. He sent Him to be born in a stable amongst animals and hay. He who came in a humble way has changed the world more than anyone else in all of history. He has revealed Himself to us and taught us about the heavenly Father.

To all who receive Jesus, those who believe in His name, God has given the right to become the children of God! We are God's children—children with access to the Father through Christ. We are born of God and are given new life. Jesus said, "I am the way, and the truth and the life. No one comes to the Father except through me" (John 14:6).

"Look! The virgin will conceive a child! She will give birth to a son, and he will be called Immanuel (meaning, God is with us)" (Matthew 1:23).

What love of God to send His only Son to save us and be "God with us."

Daily Requests

- Ask God to draw our neighborhoods to Christ and supply the workers that are needed.

- Thank God for the gift of Jesus for the salvation of all.

- Ask God to bring national repentance.

Jesus, we ask You to draw our neighborhoods to Christ. Be real to them and touch their hearts with the love of God.

Paul and Barnabas

> "Paul and Barnabas appointed elders for them in each church and, with prayer and fasting, committed them to the Lord, in Whom they had put their trust" (Acts 14:23).

The leaders chose elders in each church body to direct the church and oversee it. Then, with prayer and with fasting, they entrusted these people to the Lord "in whom they had put their trust." Even there, the apostles trusted the Lord to oversee those who were chosen to lead the local church. They prayed, fasted, and then trusted.

We must trust God's guiding hand upon the leaders that are chosen and appointed. We are all able to fail. We need God's directing hand upon us to do what He calls us to do.

Paul and Barnabas also prayed for the leaders. We must pray for the leaders in the flock and in our nation that God will have His hand upon them and work godliness into their lives and decisions. We must pray for those in leadership over us. We may even fast for them. Then we must entrust them into the care of the Lord. He is able to choose who He wants to put in that position and is able to work in their lives and convict them of sin. Our responsibility is to ask.

Daily Requests

- Pray that we would be open to God's leading and that His timing will be followed well.

- Ask God to raise up godly people in the body of Christ to lead us.

- Pray for the lost to see the love of God in our lives and be drawn, "wooed," to Him. Ask God to bring spiritual awakening in our nation.

Lord God, we ask that You would reveal Your love through our lives to the unsaved. We ask that You would draw and woo them to Yourself by Your Spirit.

God Saves

> "I cry out to God Most High, to God, who
> fulfills [His purpose] for me. He sends from
> heaven and saves me, rebuking those who hotly
> pursue me; "Selah" God sends His love and His
> faithfulness" (Psalms 57:2-3).

David wrote this Psalm when he fled from King Saul into the cave. It was like a stronghold for him where he could hide and be protected. How difficult it must have been to be chased by a king and his men. He cries out to God Most High who is over and above all, for our God is sovereign over all the affairs of men. It is He who fulfills His purpose for us. If we run from God, we will have difficulties in our lives. If we run to God, we make Him our stronghold, and He is on our side.

If God be for us, who can be against us? If we run with God and to God, He saves us and hides us in His wing. If we run away from Him, we eventually have pain that will cause us to turn around.

Fear God—not man. Fear God and not the devil. It is God who saves. It is He who performs all things for us. It is He who saves us. What has God called you to do?

Daily Requests

- Pray for a willing heart to obey and actions that follow.

- Ask God to put in us a devotion to Christ and to love with a pure heart.

- Pray for national repentance, that God will draw people to Himself and reveal truth in the nation.

Lord, we ask that You would give us the willingness of heart to obey You and the actions to follow through.

Kingdom of Heaven

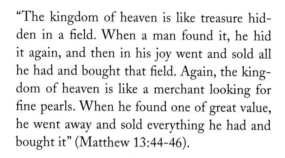

"The kingdom of heaven is like treasure hidden in a field. When a man found it, he hid it again, and then in his joy went and sold all he had and bought that field. Again, the kingdom of heaven is like a merchant looking for fine pearls. When he found one of great value, he went away and sold everything he had and bought it" (Matthew 13:44-46).

Have you ever found something of great value? Do you remember when you first came to Christ and the difference that it made? The kingdom of heaven is God's rule and reign in the universe. Personally applied, it is accepting Jesus as our Savior and Lord and living under God's rule. Obedience to God is His rule and reign in our lives. God gives the principles to live by. He guides and we follow.

What is the most valuable treasure that we could find? Is it our relationship with Jesus Christ, to find freedom in Christ, and to be a part of the body of Christ? We come to Christ, and He is our Savior and Lord and brings us into the family of God. Following God is worth everything. Is there something God wants you to let go of?

Daily Requests

- Pray for an understanding of God's will in our lives.

- Pray that the lost will come to salvation, that the eyes of their understanding will be opened.

- Ask God to guide and direct the leaders in the nation and to convict them of sin.

Lord, we ask that You would bring the lost to salvation. Open the eyes of their understanding to You and to the truth of Your Word.

Keep Your Confidence

"Do not throw away this confident trust in the Lord, no matter what happens. Remember the great reward it brings you!" (Hebrews 10:35, NLT).

"So do not throw away your confidence; it will be richly rewarded" (Hebrews 10:35).

We all have seasons when we become discouraged. But the Word of God tells us to keep our confidence, for it will be richly rewarded. There is no substitute for God's rewards. The rewards that He gives are blessings beyond what we can find on our own.

He knows the past and the present, and is fully aware of the future. We place our confidence and our assurance in God and what He has planned for us. He has a reward if we continue to pray and continue to walk with Him in obedience. Do not give up. God is good. We may not see the reward yet, but we believe. The reward will surely come, and it will be a good reward—well worth the time. He often brings blessings into our life when we obey that we do not foresee or expect. God's rewards follow our confident trust and obedience.

This world is passing away, but the kingdom of God and what is done for God's glory will last.

Daily Requests

- Ask God to dwell in us richly, that we will keep our confidence and continue to obey.

- Pray that we as a body of Christ will trust in the Lord and do good.

- Ask God to pour out His Spirit upon leaders in the nation and draw them to love God as their first love.

Lord, we ask that You would pour out Your Spirit upon the leaders in the nation. We ask that You draw them to love You with all their heart, mind, and soul.

Feeding the Four Thousand

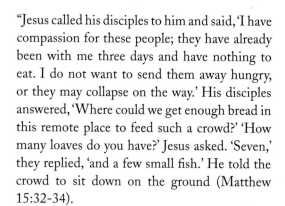

"Jesus called his disciples to him and said, 'I have compassion for these people; they have already been with me three days and have nothing to eat. I do not want to send them away hungry, or they may collapse on the way.' His disciples answered, 'Where could we get enough bread in this remote place to feed such a crowd?' 'How many loaves do you have?' Jesus asked. 'Seven,' they replied, 'and a few small fish.' He told the crowd to sit down on the ground (Matthew 15:32-34).

Can you imagine finding seven loaves and a few fish with which to feed the crowd? The crowd of four thousand had been with Jesus for three days and had nothing to eat. Jesus had compassion on them. He cared for them. Jesus told the crowd to sit down, He gave thanks for what He had, He broke it, and He gave it to the disciples to hand out to the crowd that numbered four thousand men plus women and children.

How often have you seen seven loaves of bread and a few small fish feed so many people? And it says that they all ate and were satisfied. In fact, the disciples picked up seven basketfuls of broken pieces that were left over. We love to see miracles. God loves to do them. Whatever you have to give to God and to help others, do not put it down or think it is little. God is able to multiply the little you have and make it enough.

Take what you have and give it to God. Do not put it down but see what He will do with it.

Daily Requests

- Ask God to multiply the little you have.

- Pray that Christians will give that it shall be given to them. Ask God to bring provision into the kingdom.

- Pray for the nation to draw back to God in heart, mind, soul, and spirit.

Father in heaven, we ask that You would bring provision into the kingdom and into things that You have ordained.

Serve God

> "No servant can serve two masters. Either he
> will hate the one and love the other, or he will be
> devoted to the one and despise the other. You can-
> not serve both God and money" (Luke 16:13).

The Bible talks about loving God and serving Him. It also talks about the subject of money. No one can serve two masters. What is it that tempts us to leave our first love for God? Money is definitely one that is a temptation. We must avoid two extremes—that of hoarding, being poverty driven, or that of gluttony and overspending. Either one is something that can create bondage in our lives. The balance begins with placing God first and giving the first part of what He gives us back to Him. Giving creates in us a right attitude that helps to counter sin. It also is a way of placing God first. It leads us into freedom: freedom of heart, mind, and concerns.

What will a man gain to hoard his wealth and not give rightful place to God by giving back to Him our first fruits? God desires that we give to Him off the top of our income—our wealth. It places God as first in our lives and increases our trust in Him. He also takes into His hands the responsibility to bless us through it. Many people testify that after they began giving more to God that God increased the amount they had left over at the end of the month. He gives so that we can give more. Be faithful with what you have in finances by placing Him first and giving God the first fruits of your money.

Do not place your focus in life on money. Do not look for it first. Look for God. Serve God with your whole heart and allow Him to work out your money. In the end, you will be safer with God first. The happiness that comes with money lasts only a moment. Allow God first place.

Daily Requests

- Ask God to give us balance in money issues.

- Pray for our families to love Him first and serve Him with our whole hearts.

- Ask God to put a spirit of generosity within His people in the nation.

Lord, we ask that You place a spirit of generosity upon us, as well as upon Your people in the nation, and that we will be givers.

Redeemed by Christ

> "Why should I fear when evil days come, when wicked deceivers surround me–those who trust in their wealth and boast of their great riches? No one can redeem the life of another or give to God a ransom for them" (Psalms 49:5-7).

Life is valuable. It cannot be bought with money or riches or good works. Only the blood of Jesus is the ransom and the payment to redeem us. It was on the cross that God's Son shed His blood for the sake of many. It was His life and death that brings salvation to whoever believes in His name. No amount of money can buy someone's life or give them eternal life, but we can take the money that God has allowed us to have and use it for good. We can put it toward storing up riches in heaven where moths and rust do not destroy and thieves do not break in and steal. Do not trust in your money but trust in God who is the giver of wealth.

"For there is one God and one mediator between God and mankind, the man Christ Jesus, who gave himself as a ransom for all people" (1 Timothy 2:5-6a).

How often we value riches and wealth, but what can it buy in the great scheme of things but things that perish and rust and rot in this world? It is Christ who gives life.

We need homes and food. And it is a blessing from God to have our needs provided for, yet do not trust in your riches but trust in God. The greatest use of our wealth is to provide for our needs, our family, and that which outlasts us. Give to God off the top of your wealth and allow Him to use it to bring others to Christ. Trust in God rather than wealth.

Daily Requests

- Pray for counsel to use wealth for good.

- Pray for our families and loved ones to love God more.

- Ask God to draw us into His presence and to pour out His Spirit on our nation.

Lord, we ask for our families and loved ones to love You more and place You before wealth and riches.

For Your Name's Sake

> "For your name's sake, Lord, preserve my life; in your righteousness, bring me out of trouble. "In your unfailing love, silence my enemies; destroy all my foes, for I am your servant" (Psalms 143:11-12).

David appeals to God with "for Your name's sake." God chose David to be the future king, and now because of it, David has enemies that he needs God to rescue him from. David appeals to God to preserve his life. Because of God's call to be king, he now needs intervention. He needs God to reveal His faithfulness.

A principle through the Bible is "where God calls, He also provides." David went on to ask God to silence his enemies and destroy all of his foes. Have you ever asked God to do that for you? Whether it is spiritual enemies or people who have spoken ill about you, you can ask God to do this for you, as well. Ask God to silence your enemies. Ask Him to preserve your life and bring you out of trouble. Read it as a prayer to God.

In the verses before this, David prays, "Teach me to do your will, for you are my God; may your good Spirit lead me on level ground" (Psalms 143:10).

Daily Requests

- Ask God to correct you where needed.

- Pray for God's grace and goodness to be revealed in our lives.

- Ask God to guide the decisions and hearts of leaders in the nation and to draw them to do what is pleasing to Him.

Father in heaven, we ask You to guide and direct the decisions and hearts of the leaders in the nation and draw them to act in ways that are pleasing to You.

Parable of the Net

"Once again, the kingdom of heaven is like a net that was let down into the lake and caught all kinds of fish. When it was full, the fishermen pulled it up on the shore. Then they sat down and collected the good fish in baskets, but threw the bad away. This is how it will be at the end of the age. The angels will come and separate the wicked from the righteous and throw them into the fiery furnace, where there will be weeping and gnashing of teeth" (Matthew 13:47-50).

A time is coming when God will judge the righteous and the unrighteous. Each will be judged according to his or her works. Not everyone will see heaven.

We see all kinds of people in church. Some will go to heaven. Some will not. Those who are genuine in their love for God, who have accepted the payment Jesus made for their sins and have made Jesus Christ their Lord and Savior, will be in heaven with God. How can you be among them in heaven? Ask God to forgive you for your sins. Tell God that you accept Jesus as your Lord and Savior and His gift of dying on the cross to pay for your sins. Make a personal commitment to follow Jesus.

God is the one who sees the heart and knows what is inside of a man or woman. He is the One who knows who has accepted Jesus and who has not. He is the righteous Judge that judges who is saved and who loves Him and who does not.

What is our call in life? It is to love God and to do good. We are called to place God on the throne of our lives as Lord. Then we are to act on it. Remember that God still loves those who do not know Him. They will have an eternity separated from Him. Reach out to those around you with the love of God. Pray for them, as well.

Daily Requests

- Pray for family members who do not know Christ that God's Spirit will work in their lives and break down barriers that stop them from coming to Christ.

- Ask God to teach us to do His will that we may know and abide with Him.

- Ask God to draw people in the nation back to Him as their Lord and Savior.

Lord, draw people in this nation back to You and in love with You as their Lord and Savior. Open eyes to see and hearts to receive Your love and truth.

Jesus Healed Many

"Jesus left there and went along the Sea of
Galilee. Then he went up on a mountainside
and sat down. Great crowds came to him, bringing the lame, the blind, the crippled, the mute
and many others, and laid them at his feet; and
he healed them. The people were amazed when
they saw the mute speaking, the crippled made
well, the lame walking and the blind seeing…"
(Matthew 15:29-31).

Jesus sat down. And great crowds came bringing their
friends, family, or acquaintances to Jesus and laying them
at his feet. I find it interesting that the crippled and needy
had people help them to Jesus. Even while sitting down
on the mountain, Jesus was followed by crowds and was in
the business of healing people.

What would it have been like to be there in that day?

How amazed we are in our days to see the mute able to
speak, the crippled made well, the lame able to walk, and
the blind able to see? Miracles never grow old. We have
a good and loving God who loves to heal. At times, He
works through others to bring it about. And praise God
for that.

He is the God who saves. He is the God who is able.

Daily Requests

- Pray for salvation for the lost—the eyes of their understanding to be opened to the truth of God's Word and the light of salvation in their soul.

- Ask God to heal you and your family of every sickness.

- Pray for a manifestation of God's presence in your area.

Father in heaven, we ask that you would bring unbelievers to salvation. Open the eyes of their understanding and give them revelation of truth and Your Word.

Love and Obey God

> "'Go,' the Lord said to me, 'and lead the people on their way, so that they may enter and possess the land I swore to their ancestors to give them.' And now, Israel, what does the Lord your God ask of you but to fear the Lord your God, to walk in obedience to Him, to love Him, to serve the Lord your God with all your heart and with all your soul, and to observe the Lord's commands and decrees that I am giving you today for your own good?" (Deuteronomy 10:11-13).

Many times through the Bible, God tells us that obedience to Him, to follow Him and love Him, brings blessings. Disobedience brings the opposite. It is a natural law. Sin brings death. Obedience brings life. Accepting Christ as our Lord and Savior brings life. Jesus said, "I am the Way, the Truth, and the Life" (John 14:6). He is the one that leads us and guides us. Coming to Christ brings salvation.

How great is the love of God that He gave us Christ to redeem us from sin and to lead us into true life? The commandments that God has given are for our own good. First John 2:5 says, "But if anyone obeys His Word, love for God is truly made complete in them." Are we ever perfect? No, we are human. But we have the Spirit of the living God in us to enable us and to guide us. Our obedience to God is proof of our love for Him.

Is God calling you to step out in faith and help someone? Obey. You will be blessed.

Daily Requests

- Ask God to enable us to obey and love Him.

- Pray for love to abound in the body of Christ.

- Ask God to bring truth and humility to leaders in the nation.

Lord, we ask You to give us open hearts to You, quickness to obey, and understanding of what You want us to do.

Love Deeply

> "Now that you have purified yourselves by obeying the truth so that you have sincere love for each other, love one another deeply, from the heart" (1 Peter 1:22).

> "Let Israel say: 'His love endures forever.' Let the house of Aaron say: 'His love endures forever.' Let those who fear the Lord say: 'His love endures forever'" (Psalms 118:2-4).

First, we are to purify ourselves by obedience to truth so that we have a genuine love for one another. We are not to love one another only on the surface but rather with a genuine love that flows deeply from the heart. What is the difference between surface love and deep love? There are a number of differences. The first that comes to mind here is the commitment to love. When we love deeply, we are concerned not only with our welfare but with the other person's. Deep love is a commitment, and genuine concern for the other person.

God's love is enduring. It continues. We are human and make mistakes. We quit at times. But God doesn't. He is the one who teaches us or shows us how to love. As we grow in love, we grow in our likeness to Christ.

Daily Requests

- Ask God to reveal His love for us.

- Pray for love to abound more in more in families in all knowledge and depth of insight. (Philippians 1:10)

- Pray for God to work in the hearts of the men in our nation that they might turn to godliness.

Lord, we ask that You would increasingly reveal Your love for us that we as the body of Christ would know how deep, how wide, and how high the love of Christ is.

The Lost Son

"Jesus continued: 'There was a man who had two sons. The younger one said to his father, "Father, give me my share of the estate." So he divided his property between them. 'Not long after that, the younger son got together all he had, set off for a distant country and there squandered his wealth in wild living. After he had spent everything, there was a severe famine in that whole country, and he began to be in need…'"

The story continues to say that he started feeding pigs and was hungry enough to eat their food but didn't receive even a piece of the pig's food. Then he realized that he was starving and that his father's servants were provided for far better than he was. So he returned to his father's home and planned to be a servant.

"'…But while he was still a long way off, his father saw him and was filled with compassion for him; he ran to his son, threw his arms around him and kissed him'" (Luke 15:11-14, 20).

Do we ever run back to God when we have a felt need? Of course! How often do people ignore God until they are in a situation they can't fix? Our Father in heaven longs to be with us. He longs for us to return home when we have left, and He longs for those around us to come to Him. "As a father has compassion on his children, so the Lord has compassion on those who fear him." His forgiveness is real. His love is undying. And His acceptance of us is true.

Daily Requests

- Ask God to give us understanding of His acceptance and compassion.

- Pray for God to encourage His people to stand up for Him.

- Ask God to reveal Himself in the leadership of the country!

God over all, we ask that You would touch the hearts of the leadership in the country and reveal Yourself to them and through them for Your glory and for right decisions to be made.

Ten Silver Coins

> "'Or suppose a woman has ten silver coins and loses one. Doesn't she light a lamp, sweep the house and search carefully until she finds it? And when she finds it, she calls her friends and neighbors together and says, "Rejoice with me; I have found my lost coin." In the same way, I tell you, there is rejoicing in the presence of the angels of God over one sinner who repents'" (Luke 15:8-10).

In this verse, Jesus is telling another parable about the heart of God for the lost. Each person is so valuable to God. This woman had ten silver coins and lost one. She searched high and low to find it. Do you remember the last time you searched for something valuable? And when you found it, what did you do? People are much more valuable than coins or possessions. One person's life is invaluable.

And God loves His children. When they run away, God's love never quits. His forgiveness is complete. His mercy is new every morning. And there is rejoicing in the presence of the angels of God over every person who repents. Every person who turns back to God is rejoiced over. God loved the world and gave all He could to bring us to Him. He cares that much. May we rejoice when people turn to Him and love Him wholeheartedly.

Daily Requests

- Ask God to give us compassion and His love for the lost.

- Pray for open doors of opportunity to share Him with others and for the Holy Spirit to draw people to Himself.

- Pray that people in the nation will come to love God wholeheartedly.

Holy Spirit, we pray that you will kindle a love for You in our hearts and that we will see as You see and hear as You hear.

The Lost Sheep

> "And when he finds it [the lost sheep], he joyfully puts it on his shoulders and goes home. Then he calls his friends and neighbors together and says, 'Rejoice with me; I have found my lost sheep'" (Luke 15:5-6).

God rejoices when one person comes to repentance. What is repentance? It involves the recognition of our sin and a rejection of it by moving away from it. Confession of sin is a step toward repentance, but repentance does not involve only that. We must turn away from that sin and make the immediate change, as well. God desires that everyone comes to repentance. He delights when one lost sheep (person) comes to salvation. He cares that much.

You are very important to God. He loves you and created you to be in a relationship with Him. God also cares about the lost. We, as Christians, need God's heart of compassion for others that need Christ. He sees them and loves them. We must also go and find those who are not with Christ and reveal God's goodness and love to them.

Daily Requests

- Ask God to give you compassion for those who don't know Christ.

- Pray for the body of Christ to reach out and make the most of our opportunities to love the lost and draw them to Christ.

- Pray for the leaders in your region to be trained in righteousness.

Lord God, we ask that You place within our hearts a compassion for unbelievers who don't know You and that we will reach out to them and make the most of the opportunities we have.

Seed Sown Along the Path

> "Then he told them many things in parables, saying: "A farmer went out to sow his seed. As he was scattering the seed, some fell along the path, and the birds came and ate it up…When anyone hears the message about the kingdom and does not understand it, the evil one comes and snatches away what was sown in their heart. This is the seed sown along the path" (Matthew 13:3-4, 18).

This parable could apply both to Christians and non-Christians. We hear the Word of God, the truth, which is a seed. But because of lies of the devil, that seed does not set root and grow because the evil one snatches it. Though it reached "their heart," it did not remain. The devil came and snatched what was sown. How often do people have disbelief after they hear the Word of God? At first, there is belief. Then the enemy whispers lies about it to them.

Remember that it is a spiritual battle and pray for faith in people who hear. Ask God to protect them from the seeds of doubt or disbelief that are sown from the evil one.

Daily Requests

- Ask God to give you understanding of His Word.

- Pray for people to be protected from the lies of the evil one and that the Word of God grows and multiplies to produce much fruit.

- Pray for people in the country to place God first and for Him to hound them into the kingdom.

Lord, we ask that You would work on the hearts and minds of people that they would turn to make You first. We pray that Your Holy Spirit would work in their lives to bring them into Your kingdom (Your rule and reign in their lives).

Seed Sown On Rocky Places

"Some fell on rocky places, where it did not have much soil. It sprang up quickly, because the soil was shallow. But when the sun came up, the plants were scorched, and they withered because they had no root…The seed falling on rocky ground refers to someone who hears the Word and at once receives it with joy. But since they have no root, they last only a short time. When trouble or persecution comes because of the world, they quickly fall away" (Matthew 13:5-6, 20-21).

This is another example of what happens when some people hear the gospel. They become excited because they receive it, understand it, and begin to grow. But because they are not established well in truth, they may wither and lose faith. They do not expect difficulties. When troubles come they fall back from the commitment. New Christians need people around them who can help them grow in Christ and establish roots.

We need to come to Christ and realize that His blessings come as we obey. The difficulties that come can cause us to grow up in our salvation when we continue. These difficulties can be used against us by the evil one to cause us to uproot and wither or they can be used by us to dig our roots in deep and lean on each other. Then the storms of this life will not restrict us from God's will. We all need each other.

Let us encourage one another and pray for one another to establish ourselves deeply and richly in Christ and in fellowship with other believers to be strengthened and healed.

Daily Requests

- Ask God to give you strength and faith to do His will.

- Pray for new Christians to receive joy and have people around them to encourage and enable them to grow in Christ!

- Pray for leaders in the nation to be drawn to godliness.

Lord, we ask for new Christians to grow in You so they can stand firm in the midst of difficulties. Give them great joy and people to encourage them.

Seed Sown Among Thorns

> "Other seed fell among thorns, which grew up and choked the plants. The seed falling among the thorns refers to someone who hears the word, but the worries of this life and the deceitfulness of wealth choke the word, making it unfruitful" (Matthew 13:7, 22).

How often do we concern ourselves with how much money we will have? What will tomorrow bring? How much do we have to do today to get through the concerns of the day? What are the worries that we contend with daily? Those things are thorns that will choke out the Word if we allow them to. Do you notice that it says the thorns "grew up"? The seeds had already grown into plants. It was after they had grown that the thorns stopped them from growing.

"For the love of money is a root of all kinds of evil" (1 Timothy 6:10a).

In a culture that views wealth as success, people naturally always want more. The more you have, the more you think you need. When does a person ever reach enough with wealth? Have you ever read this passage and asked the Lord if you have struggled with wrong priorities?

Daily Requests

- Ask God to enable us to seek first His kingdom and His righteousness.

- Ask God to draw non-Christians to Christ so that they will be open hearted to the truth of God's Word.

- Pray for families in the nation to be strengthened and grow in Christ-likeness.

Lord God, we ask that You would turn our hearts back to You and show us how to seek first Your kingdom and Your righteousness.

Seed Sown On Good Soil

> "Still other seed fell on good soil, where it pro-
> duced a crop—a hundred, sixty or thirty times
> what was sown. Whoever has ears, let them
> hear. But the seed falling on good soil refers to
> someone who hears the word and understands
> it. This is the one who produces a crop, yielding
> a hundred, sixty or thirty times what was sown"
> (Matthew 13:8-9, 23).

What would "good soil" refer to? One of the things God
looks for is people who are "open hearted," meaning soft
hearted and ready to receive. Sometimes people are at the
point where the gospel falls into their heart and produces
crops immediately. It falls onto soil or a life that is ready
and open. There is a need for God, or there are times
when people are ready to receive the gospel.

As Christians, we also must tend to our hearts, so that
our soil will be good and produce good fruit. How do
we do this? We ask God to help. We choose our attitude
toward situations that come. When we feel a hardness of
heart or bitterness beginning in our heart, we must talk it
out, pray it out, and change it out.

Daily Requests

- Ask God to tenderize our hearts to Him and help us be open hearted, willing to receive His Word.

- Pray for the body of Christ to love one another and produce good fruit.

- Ask God to bring national repentance so that people will make God their first priority.

Lord, we ask that You bring national repentance so that people will love You first and make You their first priority.

No Record of Sins

> "If you, Lord, kept a record of sins, Lord, who could stand? But with you there is forgiveness, so that we can, with reverence, serve you...I wait for the Lord, my whole being waits, and in his word I put my hope" (Psalms 13:3-5).

God is righteous and yet forgiving. If He kept a record of your sins, would you be able to stand? No one could. But God forgives. There is no sin that He is unable to forgive. There is no sin that He is not willing to forgive. He desires that we are close to Him. His Son paid the price for all of our sins.

His will is that no one should perish but all come to eternal life. God is kind. He is love. He desires to forgive and remove the breach in our relationship with Him that sin tends to bring. How great is our God! How great is His love and forgiveness! Remember how much He has done for us. Give back to God out of love for Him, and serve Him.

Daily Requests

- Ask God to reveal His love and mercy to us.

- Pray that God will reveal His love and forgiveness to those who don't know that He loves them.

- Pray for the nation and that Christians will lead with wisdom, counsel, and understanding.

Lord, we ask that You would raise up Christians that will lead with godly wisdom, counsel, and understanding.

Zacchaeus, Come Down

> "He [Zacchaeus] was a chief tax collector and was wealthy. He wanted to see who Jesus was, but because he was short he could not see over the crowd" (Luke 19:2-3).

Zacchaeus was eager to see Jesus. He must not have seen him before since it says, "He wanted to see who Jesus was." After all the talk of the people about Him and the miracles that He has done, he had a need to see for himself. So Luke tells us that he ran ahead and climbed a sycamore-fig tree to see him.

"When Jesus reached the spot, he looked up and said to him, "'Zaccheus, come down immediately. I must stay at your house today'" (Luke 19:5).

As the story goes, people then began to mutter that Jesus went to Zacchaeus's house, who was known for being a sinner. Tax collectors in those days were typically greedy, dishonest and rejected by people. But God knew his heart. Zaccheus changed his heart and decided to give half of his possessions to the poor and right the wrongs he had committed. His actions revealed his change of heart.

Jesus then told him "Today salvation has come to this house…"

Daily Requests

- Ask God to direct our paths.

- Ask God to bring salvation to family that needs it.

- Pray that God will direct the paths of leaders in the nation.

Lord, we lift up family that has not accepted Jesus as their Lord and Savior. We ask that You do whatever it takes in their lives to bring them to salvation.

Raised to Life

> "When he heard this, Jesus said, 'This sickness
> will not end in death. No, it is for God's glory
> so that God's Son may be glorified through it'"
> (John 11:4).

Jesus spoke this concerning Lazarus. Lazarus was sick,
and he died. His two sisters sent a message to Jesus to
come to heal him, but Jesus waited and after two days
went back to Judea where the Jews had recently tried to
stone Him. When He arrived, Lazarus had been in the
tomb—dead—for four days.

Jesus said to Lazarus' sister, "I am the resurrection and
the life. The one who believes in me will live, even though
they die; and whoever lives by believing in me will never
die. Do you believe this?" (John 11:25).

Jesus must have seemed very late to Lazarus' family.
He arrived four days after Lazarus died. Why would He
wait so long to heal his friend? God had a plan. He used
it for good in that Jesus raised Lazarus from the dead.
Rather than healing this man while he was still sick, He
revealed the ability of God to raise the dead to life.

Do you need life? Ask God to lead you into life.

Daily Requests

- Ask God to lead us into life and faith in Him.

- Pray for God's love to abound in the body of Christ and that people will see and believe.

- Ask God to bring His life into the nation through righteousness, godliness, and prayer!

Lord, we ask You to pour Your love into Christians that we will experience Your love and become Your hands and feet to reveal it to those around us.

Lust of the Eyes

"For everything in the world—the lust of the flesh, the lust of the eyes, and the pride of life— comes not from the Father but from the world" (1 John 2:16).

"Do not lust in your heart after her beauty or let her captivate you with her eyes. For a prostitute can be had for a loaf of bread" (Proverbs 6:25).

What do we allow our eyes to dwell on? We are told not to lust in our heart or allow ourselves to be captivated with our eyes by an adulteress or wayward person. The scripture says "woman," but it applies to both sexes. Keep yourself pure in thought and in heart. That is one application of avoiding lust of the eyes.

Another temptation involves fine clothes, fine hair, fine jewelry, and fine housing. These are appealing to the flesh. They are appealing to the eyes. To behold them is something that can become consuming. It is not wrong to have them. It *is* wrong to allow our desire for them to be out of balance. Focus on Christ and becoming Christ-like. Then the pride and lust of the world for such as these becomes a non issue because our heart and mind and eyes are set first on Christ.

Daily Requests

- Ask God to open our eyes to truth, wisdom, and understanding.

- Pray for truth to come in the body of Christ.

- Ask God to bring godly leaders forward in the nation to be examples and witnesses for Him.

Lord God, we ask that You bring forth leaders who are godly in the nation. We ask that You would give them courage to be godly examples and witnesses for You.

The Gift of God

> "For God saved us and called us to live a holy life—not because of anything we have done but because of His own purpose and grace. This grace was given us in Christ Jesus before the beginning of time, but it has now been revealed through the appearing of our Savior, Christ Jesus, who has destroyed death and has brought life and immortality to light through the gospel" (2 Timothy 1:9-10).

Praise God for saving us and calling us to live a holy life. What is a holy life? It is a life that is set apart for God. It is a life that involves purity and devotion to Christ. We are chosen by God and set apart for fellowship with Him. And this happened not by anything that we did. We did not earn it. We did not do enough good works to receive it. Christ paid the price on the cross at Calvary and offered the gift of new life. His own purpose and grace was to bring us near to Him, to know Him, and to receive life abundant, anew, and rich. Unbelievers do not see and experience it.

Christ Jesus also destroyed death. We do not have to fear it anymore because of the hope that we have in Christ—both in this life and in the next! We have great hope because of God's gift of salvation. Praise God today for the hope that we have in Him.

Daily Requests

- Ask God to direct our paths and guide us into purity and holiness—Christ-likeness.

- Pray for salvation for the lost and that God will open their spiritual eyes of understanding.

- Ask God to strengthen and purify leadership in the country.

Lord God, we ask that You would purify and strengthen the key people in leadership in the country. Draw them to what is right.

Honesty

"I call on the Lord in my distress, and he answers me. Save me, Lord, from lying lips and from deceitful tongues" (Psalms 120:1-2).

"The Lord detests lying lips, but he delights in people who are trustworthy" (Proverbs 12:22).

Have you ever had people lie to you or about you? Have you experienced someone spreading rumors about you? Is it because you are a Christian or because you stood your ground? Here the psalmist called on God in his trouble. You are not the only one who has difficulty with someone lying to you or being deceitful. Sooner or later in life, it happens to everyone.

The psalmist had faith that God would deal with the lies. Psalms 120 goes on to say of the liar, "He will punish you with a warrior's sharp arrows, with burning coals of the broom bush." God hates dishonesty. There are consequences for it. So, what is a "broom bush"? It is similar to the invasive American plant known as a *noxious weed*. It becomes dense and costs millions of dollars of lost timber production. Lies have a way of accumulating if not dealt with. Like weeds, they begin to run beyond our plans and overrun in business or life if not removed. Honesty is the best policy (with love, of course).

Be honest with love. Allow God to deal with the consequences.

Daily Requests

- Ask God to direct our thoughts and lives into truth with love.

- Pray for honesty with love in the body of Christ and God's blessings upon it.

- Ask God to raise up godly leaders in the nation, who recognize deceit and choose truth.

Lord, we ask that You direct our thoughts and lives into truth with love. Strengthen us in truth and love.

Always Awake

> "I lift up my eyes to the mountains, where does my help come from? My help comes from the Lord, the Maker of heaven and earth. He will not let your foot slip—he who watches over you will not slumber; indeed, he who watches over Israel will neither slumber nor sleep" (Psalms 121:1-4).

God, who watches over you, never sleeps. He never says, "Come back later, I am too busy." He is always watching over us. He provides for our needs and at times may encourage us to go to others, as well, because He made the body of believers to encourage and help one another. He can work through other people as well.

Nevertheless, He is the one person who is always there and is always awake to help. He who made the heaven and earth (and you and me) also has good plans and ways to help us when we cry out to Him. His arm is not too short to save (Numbers 11:23). Have you ever wondered if He could save you?

Remember the Lord when you need help or feel alone.

Daily Requests

- Pray for God to remind you of His love and faithfulness and reveal Himself to you.

- Ask God to comfort the lonely with His presence and remind them of His love.

- Pray for leaders in the nation to turn to God for help and realize He is always there.

God, we ask that You reveal Yourself as always present and the One that can help people in the nation, that we will run to You.

Love for the Lost

> "When Jesus landed and saw a large crowd, he had compassion on them, because they were like sheep without a shepherd. So he began teaching them many things" (Mark 6:34).

How many people are looking for fulfillment and direction in life but cannot find it because they have no one to show them how to find it? We have all these external goals in life to try to fill our voids: clothes, furniture, career, relationships, etc. They are all needed to some extent, but when God is left out, there is a missing piece in our lives. If you feel you are missing something, ask yourself if you have left God out of the sequence.

Jesus saw the crowd and had compassion on them. He took time for them and taught them. We all need teaching to grow in Christ—the teaching of the Word. Jesus was compassionate on the people's needs. He and the disciples were planning to rest when the crowd started following Him. He saw the need and the people were eager to hear.

Go out of your way to reach someone for Christ. Have compassion on them and take the time to share Christ with them.

Daily Requests

- Pray for God to guide us into lives that are like Jesus.

- Pray for compassion for the lost to come upon God's people.

- Ask God to raise up godliness in the nation to draw people to Him.

Lord, we ask that You would release Your people from temporal values and concerns and that we will be mission minded for the glory of Christ and have compassion for the lost. Give us Your heart for those who don't know You.

Stewardship

> "He replied, 'I tell you that to everyone who has, more will be given, but as for the one who has nothing, even what they have will be taken away'" (Luke 19:26).

In this parable, Jesus spoke of a man who entrusted different amounts of money (called talents or minas) to three different people. As the people proved faithful, he entrusted them with more. The last one took his one talent and buried it in the ground and did nothing with it but hide it. He is the one who had his talent, or mina, taken away from him. It was then given to the one who had been faithful with his money.

The principle Jesus gives here is stewardship. He gives us various gifts, money, and abilities. We are not to hide them or bury them but rather to use and invest what we have been given for Him.

What we do with what God has given to us is our responsibility.

Around 1958, a Plymouth Belvedere car was buried in the ground in concrete with the hopes of preserving it. After fifty years, it was pulled up. When the lid was popped off the container, all that was visible was the roof of the car. The rest had been sitting in water, and it completely ruined the car. All that was left was a "rust bucket."

What are the gifts that God has given to you to use for Him?

Daily Requests

- Ask God to help us be responsible with and use what He has given to us.

- Ask God to draw sinners to repentance and reveal His love to them.

- Pray that leaders will be faithful with the gifts and abilities that God has given to them.

Lord, we ask that You would stimulate Your people to use the gifts that You have given to us and that we will be faithful and develop the gifts that You give to us. We ask for passion and desire to use them in godly ways that will help to make a difference in our communities, families, and nation.

Believe

> "The jailer called for lights, rushed in and fell trembling before Paul and Silas. He then brought them out and asked, 'Sirs, what must I do to be saved?' They replied, 'Believe in the Lord Jesus, and you will be saved—you and your household.' Then they spoke the word of the Lord to him and to all the others in his house" (Acts 16:29-32).

As the story goes, Paul and Silas were thrown into prison for helping a girl who was possessed by an evil spirit. In the midst of the situation, Paul and Silas "were praying and singing hymns to God." All of a sudden, there was such a violet earthquake that the prison doors flew open and everyone's chains came loose.

How often do we praise God in the midst of difficult situations? During their praying and singing, God sent a miracle and set them free. The jailer asked what he must do to be saved, and they gave the simplest reply. "Believe in the Lord Jesus, and you will be saved…" The way to salvation is simple. Believe and follow Christ in a decided dedication. Allow God to lead your paths. Believe in the Lord Jesus, and you will be saved.

KARI BITZ

The word salvation in the original language refers to more than just "saved." It applies to more than eternal salvation. It also refers to deliverance, safety, preservation, deliverance from danger, and apprehension. It is a word that describes the grace of God. Believe on the Lord Jesus Christ, and you shall be saved. Follow Him and obey.

Daily Requests

- Ask God to direct your paths.

- Ask God to bring unbelievers to a saving knowledge of Jesus Christ.

- Pray for people in the nation to be drawn back to their Christian heritage.

Father in heaven, we ask that You guide us and direct our paths according to what is best. We ask that we will have faith and courage to follow You.

The Light of Life

> "In Him (Jesus) was life, and that life was the light of all mankind. The light shines in the darkness, and the darkness has not overcome it" (John 1:4-5).

Jesus came to earth to give life to us. His desire was to restore joy and peace in our lives as well as bring us into true life. Without Christ, we are spiritually dead. We are dead in sin without the understanding of what we need in Christ and without understanding our sin. It is with Christ and the Holy Spirit who lives in us when we accept Christ as our Lord and Savior that we are ushered into life. It is life anew.

Jesus loves to give life to people. People who are down and out need the light of Christ in their lives to give them hope for eternal life. With Christ, your future and your present change.

Jesus said in John 8:12, "I am the light of the world. Whoever follows me will never walk in darkness, but will have the light of life." Jesus has come to reveal truth. This truth shines in the darkness and brings us into life. Bringing secrets, feelings, and misunderstandings into the open offers healing, truth, and life to be brought into our lives.

Daily Requests

- Pray that God will open our eyes, ears, heart, and will to accept His light and life.

- Ask God to shine His light into homes across the nation to draw people to Him.

- Pray that people will come to know the truth of God's Word and be open to His leading in the nation and in the leadership of the nation.

Lord, we ask You to reveal and shine Your light and truth into homes across the nation. Draw people to You to accept You as Lord.

Prayer

> "Yet the news about Him spread all the more, so that crowds of people came to hear him and to be healed of their sicknesses. But Jesus often withdrew to lonely places and prayed" (Luke 5:15-16).

How often did Jesus withdraw to lonely places to pray? Jesus prayed often. He withdrew from the crowds and people who followed Him to spend time in prayer with the Father. This is an example to us. In the midst of our busy schedules, we must take time to pray. Make the effort to withdraw from the busyness and people to pray often.

I have heard people say, "We all have the same amount of time in a day." It's how we prioritize or use the time that makes a difference. If we do not have the time now, why would we have the time later? We must make the effort now. Carve out the time from your schedule to spend with the most important person in the universe—the Creator and God of it all.

Daily Requests

- Ask God to guide you and direct you in His ways and to place Him first in everything.

- Ask God to draw His children to spend time with Him in prayer often.

- Ask God to convict hearts of sin and righteousness in the nation and for people to be drawn to godliness.

Lord, we ask that You open our eyes to the power of prayer. Increase our faith in prayer and guide us into Your will.

Love of God

> "But you, Lord, are a compassionate and gracious God, slow to anger, abounding in love and faithfulness. "Turn to me and have mercy on me; show your strength in behalf of your servant; save me, because I serve you just as my mother did" (Psalms 86:15-16).

Our God is a compassionate God. He is full of grace and patience. He is abounding in love and faithfulness. He is true. He is right. He is the God who saves. This psalm is a prayer of David. He begins the psalm by saying, "Hear me, Lord, and answer me, for I am poor and needy. Guard my life, for I am faithful to you…"

Do you ever have times that you feel a need like that for God to work? David did, too. God is with you and loves to reveal Himself to you. He is the God who forgives and casts your sin as far as the east is from the west. David cried out to God for help many times and was honest with Him. Cry out to God. Pray to Him on your behalf and on behalf of those around you. He is a God who saves.

God, we pray that You will glorify Your name. Turn to us and have mercy on us. Show your strength and save us because we serve you.

Daily Requests

- Ask God to direct our paths.

- Pray for Israel and that God will protect, strengthen, and reveal Himself to them.

- Ask God to manifest His presence in the nation and reveal Himself in mighty ways.

Jehovah Jireh, we ask that You would protect and strengthen Israel. Reveal Yourself to the people in Israel in a mighty way.

Lust of the Flesh

"But if you bite and devour one another, beware lest you be consumed by one another! I say then: Walk in the Spirit, and you shall not fulfill the lust of the flesh. For the flesh lusts against the Spirit, and the Spirit against the flesh; and these are contrary to one another, so that you do not do the things that you wish" (Galatians 5:15-17, NKJV).

Do you ever do what you don't want to do? How often do we feel pulled in two directions? God's Word says, "Walk in the Spirit." What does it mean to "walk in the Spirit"? To be led by the Spirit of God is to obey God. We obey Him rather than what our natural desires, tendencies, and flesh want us to do.

The flesh includes our sinful nature. The desire to make ourselves first is one fruit of the flesh. It would also include adultery and sexual sin, hatred, contentions, jealousies, rage, and selfishness. (For more, see Galatians 5:19-21.)

We are not to follow what our flesh desires but rather what God desires. The first thing God desires is to love God. The second is to love one another. Sin entices, but in the end it leads to separation from God.

Do not obey your natural flesh desires, but rather obey God. It takes effort, but in obedience to God, we find the greatest blessings and rich rewards!

Daily Requests

- Pray that your words will be loving toward one another!

- Ask God to draw Christians into purity and that unbelievers around will see the example of Christ through our lives.

- Pray for the nation to turn back to God.

Lord, we ask that Your powerful hand would raise up godly pastors and leaders who are encouraged and full of passion for You.

Generosity

"One man gives freely, yet gains even more" (Proverbs 11:24).

"Give, and it will be given to you: good measure, pressed down, shaken together, and running over will be put into your bosom. For with the same measure that you use, it will be measured back to you" (Luke 6:38, NKJV).

This second verse falls in a discourse about not judging others. It says, "Judge not…," condemn not, forgive. Then it comes to "give." How many people have more *after* giving compared to before they gave? God gives us wealth and success to use it for His kingdom rather than for our pride or arrogance. I once heard a story of a man who started a business and made God a partner in it. He began giving from the business to God and gradually increased his giving to most of the wealth the business brought in each year.

The business grew to a large size after a time. The owner was still able to take out a decent salary—enough to live on. Even though he was in the business world, his ministry was distributing his wealth into God's kingdom.

There is freedom that comes with giving. It blesses the giver and the kingdom of God. We do not always know what people are giving to God. Giving brings joy and enables us to enjoy what God has given us without succumbing to gluttony or flesh.

Stretch yourself this month to give!

Daily Requests

- Pray that God will give us a giving heart and attitude.

- Pray that Christians will be generous and reveal Christ's love for others.

- Ask God to soften the heart of people in the nation to Him and to follow godly ways.

Lord, we ask that You will instill within us a generous heart and attitude and that we will be generous with those who have needs and meet them with the love of Christ.

Grace and Love

> "Now our Lord Jesus Christ himself, and God,
> even our Father, which hath loved us, and hath
> given us everlasting consolation and good
> hope through grace, comfort your hearts, and
> establish you in every good word and work" (2
> Thessalonians 2:16-17, NKJV).

Have you ever prayed this passage for people? Who
wouldn't want to be comforted and strengthened in heart
in every good work and word?

What does it say first? God has loved us. He loved
us before we loved Him. While we were still living in sin,
Christ died for us. Before we ever turned to Him, He
went out of His way to draw us. God revealed His love for
us in Christ and gave us comfort for this life and for the
life to come. He is the "God of all comfort, who comforts
us in all our troubles…" (2 Corinthians 1:3b-4a).

God loves you and wants to comfort you. There is
comfort in Christ.

Daily Requests

- Ask God to draw us into His love and grace and
that our hearts are comforted and strengthened in
every good word and deed.

- Pray for salvation of the lost and that the eyes of the spiritually blind would be opened and their hearts softened.

- Ask God to guide the leaders of the nation to love God and follow godliness.

Father in heaven, we ask that You bring the lost to salvation in Christ. Open the eyes of the blind and soften their hearts to receive Christ.

Grace

"What then? Shall we sin because we are not under the law but under grace? By no means!" (Romans 6:15).

As Christians, we are under grace. Yet there are natural consequences for sin. God has paid the price for our sins. His gift of sending Jesus to pay for our sins brought us into His grace. How amazing. What love of God to plan, prepare, and enact all of it by His choice to offer us a free gift. All we have to do is accept it by faith. If we choose to follow God, we are set free from the law of sin and death.

The next verse continues to say that we are servants to whomever we obey, whether of sin, which leads to death, or of obedience, which leads us to righteousness. Later on in the passage, it also says presenting ourselves to God leads to holiness and everlasting life.

John 1:17 says, "…grace and truth came through Jesus Christ."

The grace of God is unmerited favor. We are only free from sin by following God. Grace could also be understood as the sovereign influence of God at work to give restoration, new life, and strength to His people. He gives us grace, pardon, favor, gifts, and mercy when we accept His gift of salvation through faith in Jesus Christ.

We *continue* to grow up in the grace and knowledge of the Lord Jesus Christ. Thank God for His grace upon us!

Daily Requests

- Ask God to grow us up in the grace and knowledge—or truth—of Jesus Christ.

- Pray for God to work in us His saving power and grace to deliver us from our circumstances and struggles.

- Ask God to encourage His leaders in the nation in His ways and to follow after godliness.

Lord, we pray that You will stretch forth Your hand to bring encouragement to Your leaders in the nation to follow Your ways and to follow after what is good and right.

Pride of Life

"For everything in the world—the lust of the flesh, the lust of the eyes, and the pride of life—comes not from the Father but from the world" (1 John 2:16).

"To fear the Lord is to hate evil; I hate pride and arrogance, evil behavior and perverse speech" (Proverbs 8:13).

What is it about pride that God hates? Is it the attitude that we see of "I'll do what I want"? Is it the desire to run our own lives rather than allow God to lead us and direct us? Pride turns the corner to make ourselves gods rather than God. It says, "We are better." It causes one to think more highly of themselves than they ought. It is sin.

What do you think of when you think of pride? In our culture, it could be related to what size of vehicle we drive or the house that we own. Pride of life refers to boasting and arrogance, as well. We think we know better than God.

Pride and arrogance are lumped together with evil behavior and perverse speech. The opposite is to fear the Lord and hate evil. Have a healthy respect for the Lord. His ways are best. He loves us. What He plans for us is good, and His ways bring blessings.

Fear the Lord and hate evil. Avoid pride and arrogance, evil behavior, and perverse speech.

Daily Requests

- Ask that God will open our eyes to see that His ways are best.

- Pray for hope to increase in Christians and for us to have a healthy respect for the Lord.

- Ask God to tear down walls that hinder people from coming to Him in the nation.

Lord, we ask that You open our eyes to see that Your ways are best.

Guard Your Heart

"Above all else, guard your heart for everything you do flows from it" (Proverbs 4:23, NIV).

The Word tells us here to "keep" or "guard" our hearts. We must do it with diligence. Our battle is not against other people but rather against the world, the flesh, and the devil. There are times our emotions do not obey God's instructions. It is then that we adjust our attitude and do it anyway. Obedience is key.

Because of the battle that we have, we must tend our heart and care for it with diligence. Protect our hearts from sin. We battle the lust of the flesh, the lust of the eyes, and the pride of life. The possessions and temptations of this world tend to pull us in directions of making other priorities first in our lives. God tells us to love Him first. Sin can be subtle, and before we know it, it can take root or ground in our heart.

Keep your heart with diligence. Keep God first and continue to seek Him always.

Daily Requests

- Ask God to help us keep our hearts with all diligence and to guard our hearts.

- Ask God to bring unity and genuine love in the body of Christ.

- Pray for Christians in the nation to unite in prayer and in fasting.

Lord, we ask that Christians would be united in faith, love, and in mission. We ask for there to be genuine love amongst Christians and forgiveness between them.

Love and Truth

"If anyone has material possessions and sees a brother or sister in need but has no pity on them, how can the love of God be in that person? Dear children, let us not love with words or speech but with actions and in truth" (1 John 3:17-18).

God speaks here about acting upon the love of God in us. How can there be truth to love if we do not act upon it? Do we claim to love? Then our responsibility is to act in love. Give to those who need. Do not hold back because we do not believe that we have a responsibility to do it. We *do* have a responsibility. God has placed us in a family, in a neighborhood, and among coworkers and people whom we know.

Who around us is in need of help? Who lacks material possessions? Is there a family who has needs or has a difficult time meeting their bills, or is unemployed? The Word of God tells us that "God loves a cheerful giver" (2 Corinthians 9:7).

Daily Requests

- Ask God to open our eyes to the needs around us and ask for willing hearts to give.

- Ask God to stir the hearts of unbelievers to receive Christ as Lord.

- Pray for the leaders of the nation to love God.

Lord, we ask that You soften the hearts of the leaders in the nation to You and that they will make You their Lord and Savior and love You with all their heart, mind, and soul.

Gluttony

> "When you sit to dine with a ruler, note well what is before you, and put a knife to your throat if you are given to gluttony. Do not crave his delicacies, for that food is deceptive" (Proverbs 23:1-3).

The story of Daniel is a perfect example of not giving into gluttony. Daniel chose to forgo the rich food of the king when he was taken into captivity. Instead, he asked for a simple diet.

"But Daniel resolved not to defile himself with the royal food and wine, and he asked the chief official for permission not to defile himself this way" (Daniel 1:8). After a period of time, he appeared healthier than the others who were on the royal food and wine. God blessed him in his decision.

He refused to give in to the rich food of the king. So what exactly is gluttony? To eat too much, to drink too much, and to crave more. Self-control is something that God desires for us to put into practice. Eat less. Eat healthy food. Take care of our bodies and our hearts.

Daily Requests

- Pray for the self-control to live in ways that are pleasing to Him.

- Ask God to hound the lost into the kingdom and to change their minds about accepting Him as their Lord and Savior.

- Ask God to guide the leaders of the nation in godliness and honesty.

Lord, we ask that Your Holy Spirit would work and move and continue to draw the lost to You. Reveal truth to them.

White-Washed Tombs

"Blind Pharisee! First clean the inside of the cup and dish, and then the outside also will be clean. Woe to the teachers of the law and Pharisees, you hypocrites! You are like white-washed tombs, which look beautiful on the outside but on the inside are full of the bones of the dead and everything unclean" (Matthew 23:26-27).

Jesus rebuked the Pharisees for their ways. They were religious leaders who were known to follow things to the letter of the law.

Have you ever felt like your attitude has been wrong in a decision even though your actions appeared right? The Pharisees followed things to the letter of the law. They looked perfect on the outside, but Jesus said they were hypocrites. Their hearts did not match their appearance or actions.

Have you ever had a child who was outwardly compliant but inwardly rebellious? They are pretending to agree or obey but have an attitude of sin? As Christians, we are called to be genuine. God is concerned mostly with our heart. When our heart is right, the actions will follow. The Pharisees were more concerned about how they appeared to people than whether their hearts were clean. God sees the heart.

When we have a difficulty with our attitude and condition of our heart, come clean before God and even other people when needed. Ask for help and prayer. Concern yourself with the condition of your heart first, and your actions will follow. "First clean the inside of the cup and dish, and then the outside also will be clean."

Daily Requests

- Ask God to change your heart and that of your family where need be.

- Ask God to lead the churches in your region into genuineness in their love for God.

- Ask God to heal the heart of the nation and turn its ways to godliness.

Lord, we ask that You heal the heart of the nation and turn the ways of the people to godliness.

Love the Lord

> "Jesus replied, 'Love the Lord your God with all your heart and with all your soul and with all your mind'" (Matthew 22:37).

> "Love your neighbor as yourself'"" (Luke 10:27).

There are a certain number of problems that will work themselves out if we will place God first and love our neighbor. Jesus said that these are the first and greatest commandments. God gives us principles to live by. His condition is that if we will live by these principles, we will have blessings. What are blessings? They include life abundant, hope, peace, provision, sustenance, faith, grace, and God's hand working in and through our various circumstances to bring victory. We all have various needs. The first principle is to place God first.

The second principle is to "Love your neighbor as yourself." What do you do for yourself? What do you forgive yourself for that you do not forgive your neighbor for? God is calling us to love our neighbor as ourselves. Do not expect people to be perfect. Place God first in life and love others in spite of their imperfections, and He will work through our situations to bring blessing.

Daily Requests

- Ask God to manifest His presence in our communities, families, and nation.

- Pray that the body of Christ will stand united for the glory of God.

- Ask God to draw people to Christ in our nation, communities, and families.

Lord, we ask that Your Spirit would draw people to Christ in our nation, communities, and families. We ask that You draw their hearts to You.

Love and Forgiveness

"A woman in that town who lived a sinful life learned that Jesus was eating at the Pharisee's house, so she came there with an alabaster jar of perfume. As she stood behind him at his feet weeping, she began to wet his feet with her tears. Then she wiped them with her hair, kissed them and poured perfume on them…" (Luke 7:37-38).

A Pharisee asked Jesus to eat at his house. Then the Pharisee doubted Jesus for allowing this sinful woman to touch him and wash his feet (Luke 7:39). But who did Jesus defend? Was it the Pharisee or the woman who had lived a sinful life? He defended the woman who realized her need for Jesus.

Jesus goes on a couple of verses later to say, "Therefore, I tell you, her many sins have been forgiven—as her great love has shown. But whoever has been forgiven little loves little."

Have we been forgiven much? Do we love much? How often do we forget the many sins that Christ has forgiven us of? Take the time to remember and be thankful to God for His love and for His forgiveness. Remember what He has done for us. Be compassionate toward those who do not know Christ. Remember that we were once there as well. They need Christ. Pray for them and reach out to them with the love of God in word and action.

Daily Requests

- Ask God to make a way to open doors to share Christ with those around us and to open our eyes to see them.

- Ask God for confidence in sharing Christ and that what we share will take root in their lives for good.

- Ask God to open people's eyes in the nation to His goodness and grace.

Lord, we ask for courage and confidence to share Christ with others. We ask that You will speak through what we share and that it will take root in people's lives for good.

Blessings

> "Peace be to the brethren, and love with faith, from God the Father and the Lord Jesus Christ. Grace be with all those who love our Lord Jesus Christ with incorruptible love" (Ephesians 6:23-24).

Paul often ended his letters with blessings. In this chapter, he ends with a blessing again. Jesus also told His disciples, when He sent them out in Matthew 10:12, "When you are invited into someone's home, give it your blessing…" If it turns out to be a worthy home, let your blessing stand; if it is not, take back the blessing.

Jesus blessed the children when they came to Him. Mark 10:16 says, "And he [Jesus] took the children in his arms, placed his hands on them and blessed them." Jesus's disciples were going to turn these children away, but Jesus rebuked them for it. He blessed them, instead.

Blessings are powerful in the spiritual realm. I don't believe we realize the power of a blessing in our marriage, relationships, and over our children's lives. Take time, often to speak encouraging words to the people around you. Some Jewish families speak blessings over their children regularly and it shows in their achievements.

Take the time to speak blessings over people around you. It could be as simple as: "May God bless you!" Ask God to lead you into ways of blessings others.

Daily Requests

- Ask God for peace, grace, and love with faith to be upon your family, pastors, teachers, etc.

- Pray for the blessing of the Lord to be upon_____. (Fill in the blank with people's names).

- Ask God to bring conviction of sin in the judicial wing and that their choices will be God pleasing.

Lord, we ask for Your peace and grace to be upon _____. We also ask for your love with faith to be in our lives.

Speak Boldly

> "And pray on my behalf and that utterance may be given to me in the opening of my mouth, to make known with boldness the mystery of the gospel, for which I am an ambassador in chains; that in proclaiming it I may speak boldly, as I ought to speak" (Ephesians 6:19-20, NAS).

The apostle Paul had just encouraged the Christians in the previous verse to pray in the Spirit and for all believers. Then he added a request for prayer for himself, asking that they would pray that he would be bold. How often are we timid when sharing our faith in Christ? Even the apostle Paul, who was so well known for his boldness and courage, reveals his humanity. Even he may have struggled with timidity in proclaiming Christ.

How nice it is to know that we are not the only ones who have difficulty or challenges sharing our faith. Even those who seem to be able to do things easily or are known for their ability to share Christ have to overcome weaknesses in the process. Do not concern yourself with being perfect when you share—but be willing.

Then, pray these verses for your pastors, teachers, leaders, and fellow Christians in the workplace to be willing to share and have the courage and boldness to follow the Lord in it.

Daily Requests

- Ask God to give us the words and open our mouths to boldly share Christ with others as we ought.

- Pray for the seeds that we sow in the lives of others to take root and produce fruit.

- Ask God to bring revival in our nation and reveal His love and truth to people in the nation.

Lord, we ask that You will bring revival in our nation. Revive us again and reveal Your love and truth to us in a powerful way.

Pray Always

> "Put on salvation as your helmet, and take the
> sword of the Spirit, which is the Word of God;
> Pray in the Spirit at all times and on every
> occasion. Stay alert and be persistent in your
> prayers for all believers everywhere" (Ephesians
> 6:17-18, NLT).

The passage that begins even before these verses above,
about putting on the full armor of God to protect ourselves from the fiery darts or "onslaught" of the enemy,
ends with the command to pray always, especially for one
another as believers. We are to be strong in the Lord and
in the power of His might, put on the full armor of God,
and pray always.

It directs, "praying always with all prayer and supplication in the Spirit." (NKJV) We are to be alert, and pray with
perseverance and intercession for each other as believers.
We need each other.

So what is prayer? It is an open relationship with God.
It is communion. We talk to God and listen to God. We
ask of God and trust Him.

What is supplication? It is specifically "requests and
intercession on behalf of others." We are to be on our
guard—alert and watchful with perseverance in prayer.

We need each other. Prayer is a ministry. Remember to pray for your brothers and sisters in Christ and those who are being persecuted for their faith around the world!

Daily Requests

- Pray for healing to occur in the body of Christ.

- Pray for your brothers and sisters in Christ to be strengthened in Christ and for God's divine interaction in their lives.

- Ask God to bring the lost to salvation and to open their heart to Him.

Lord, we ask that You strengthen Christians in You. We will put on salvation as our helmet and take the sword of the Spirit—the Word of God—and cut through all the lies of the enemy.

Love the Lord Your God

"Love the Lord your God with all your heart, with all your soul and with all your strength" (Matthew 22:37).

"Because of your love for God, love your neighbor as yourself" (Matthew 22:39b).

Do we love our neighbor? How do we do this? Do we spend time with them? "Give and it shall be given to you" is a verse that applies to loving our neighbor as ourself. If we love God, we must also love each other, as well. Who is your neighbor? It is the person who is next to you or the person who lives close by. It also includes your coworkers and others who are around you or who you come into contact with. Let us love, for love is of God. He who loves is born of God.

The world does not know God, for it has not seen Him. But we as Christians have known God and have discovered that He is love. Let our example shine to those around us. He who loves is born of God.

Daily Requests

- Pray that our love will abound more and more for one another.

- Ask God to reveal Himself to unbelievers in miraculous ways.

- Ask God to bring Godliness in our nation.

Lord, we ask that our love would abound more and more in all knowledge and depth of insight so that we love as You love.

What is Love Like?

> "Love is patient, love is kind. It does not envy, it does not boast, it is not proud. It is not rude, it is not self-seeking, it is not easily angered, it keeps no record of wrongs" (1 Corinthians 13:4-5).

Who does all these things? We are to be walking examples to non-Christians of the way that Jesus loves us. God is love. The natural desires of man are to hold a grudge, to be self-seeking, to be rude, and to be easily angered; the list goes on. But God gives us a different example. He tells us to be like Him. Our example in our life is to shine the light of Christ's glory to others and offer them hope in Christ.

We are to forgive one another and to love one another. One of the most common sins that people struggle with is un-forgiveness. At times, we think that holding a grudge will do us good, but in the end, it leads to an open door to the enemy. It is sin.

Daily Requests
- Pray for forgiveness and love to uproot any bitterness in our lives.

- Ask God to bring unity in the body of Christ and that we will be mission-minded for His glory.

- Pray for national repentance—a massive turning in the nation for God.

Lord, we ask that You work in our hearts and lives to pour in love and uproot and remove all un-forgiveness or bitterness that is there. We ask for loving hearts that forgive.

The True God

"Now while Paul waited for them at Athens, his spirit was provoked within him when he saw that the city was given over to idols. Therefore he reasoned in the synagogue with the Jews and with the Gentile worshipers, and in the marketplace daily with those who happened to be there...Then Paul stood in the midst of the Areopagus and said, 'Men of Athens, I perceive that in all things you are very religious; for as I was passing through and considering the objects of your worship, I even found an altar with this inscription: "To the Unknown God." Therefore, the One whom you worship without knowing, Him I proclaim to you'" (Acts 17:16-17, 22-23).

Paul became angry at sin. He was provoked, and it moved him to action. When is the last time this happened to you? Do we get angry at sin? What does it drive us to do?

Many people do not know the true God or have a personal relationship with Him. What they think is right is the way of rituals, but it is the heart that God is most concerned about. He desires for our heart to be right. It is the heart that is at the center of our drives and motivations.

People need the Lord. They need us to love them, to talk with them, and to spend time with them to draw them to Christ who is the Way, the Truth, and the Life. We are supposed to love people. Hate sin when you see it. And love what is good. Paul was angry with the idolatry and chose to share the truth of Christ with the people. Reach out to those around you. Defend truth.

Daily Requests

- Open the eyes of people's understanding to know who is the true and living God.

- Draw people to Christ and open doors of opportunity for us to be witnesses to them. (Sometimes it requires spending time with them.)

- Pray for open doors of opportunity in the nation to share the gospel with others and enable them to see the truth.

Lord, we ask that you shine upon unbelievers and draw them to Christ. We ask that Your Spirit would move in their lives. Open the eyes of their understanding and open their ears to hear Your Word of truth. Open their hearts to receive You.

Do Not Grieve the Holy Spirit

> "And do not grieve the Holy Spirit of God, with whom you were sealed for the day of redemption. Get rid of all bitterness, rage and anger, brawling and slander, along with every form of malice. Be kind and compassionate to one another, forgiving each other, just as in Christ God forgave you" (Ephesians 4:30-31).

Do you know that we can cause the Holy Spirit to feel grief or sorrow? Our actions and the condition of our heart can cause the Holy Spirit to grieve.

Ephesians 4:31 says that we are to get rid of all of the sins it states, including malice of every form. What exactly is malice? It is a deep-seated meanness—a desire to injure someone. Have you ever felt that way? The Word of God says to get rid of every form of it. The descriptions before it can all be ways of getting back at people. Malice first finds its roots in bitterness and unforgiveness. It is a type of seeking revenge.

How do we forgive when someone injures us? We make a choice to do it. We can also ask God to increase our willingness to forgive. Ask God to pour love into your heart to heal and forgive through you. When it is difficult, continue to speak to that mountain daily. Continue to ask

God for His aid and continue to make the choice daily. Do not act out the temptations to get even that you have but rather submit it to God.

Be kind and compassionate to one another, just as through Christ God forgave you.

Daily Requests

- Pray for kindness and compassion to fill up our lives, families, and loved ones.

- Pray for unbelievers to know Christ, to open their eyes of understanding, and to open their ears to hear truth.

- Ask God to reveal Himself in our nation in a mighty way.

Lord, we ask that You fill up our lives, our families' lives, and our loved ones' lives with kindness and compassion.

Cords of Sin

"An evil man is held captive by his own sins; they are ropes that catch and hold him" (Proverbs 5:22, NLT).

Can you think of entanglements that sin brings? There is a reason why God has set guidelines and directives in scripture. It is not to be a kill joy. It is rather to lead us into a life that is full of abundance and peace. The Lord sees our ways. He knows what sin leads to. It leads us away from God rather than closer to Him.

Sin always appears fun for the season but in the end it brings pain and separation from God. God knows the long term effects of sin and He knows the ways it affects not only us but others around us. Hate evil. Cling to what is good and the reward will be well worth it. Ask God if there is something in your life that He wants you to deal with?

Daily Requests

- Ask God to reveal sin that you must deal with and to enable you to change where needed.

- Ask God to reveal sin in your families and to give His grace and love for them to change.

- Pray for people in our nation to be convicted of sin and to be drawn to the life-giving Spirit of God.

God, we ask that You convict people in the nation of sin and draw them to life that is in Christ through Your precious Spirit. Reveal truth and woo them to yourself.

Grounded In Love

> "(I pray) that Christ may dwell in your hearts through faith; that you, being rooted and grounded in love, may be able to comprehend with all the saints what is the width and length and depth and height to know the love of Christ which passes knowledge…" (Ephesians 3:17-19a).

What does the apostle Paul pray for? He prays first for faith: that Christ would reside in the Christian's hearts through faith so that they would be established in love. What is love? It is to act as Christ acted. It is to give when we don't feel like giving and to help when we don't want to help. It is to care about the lost, the hurting, and the blind. It is to spend our lives on behalf of others.

We are to grow together in love and to grow outward into the community with love. Is there any way for Christians to be one as God and Christ are one but with love? We must put love on. Wear it. Be rooted and established in it. Act upon it.

Daily Requests

- Ask God to reveal His love for us.

- Pray that God will restore hope to the hopeless.

- Pray that God will raise up godly people in the nation who will be bold and act in righteousness.

Lord God, we ask that You reveal the greatness of Your love for us. Open our understanding to know the height, the width, and the depth of Your love in our lives.

Do Not Fear

> "Do not be afraid of sudden terror, nor of trouble from the wicked when it comes; For the Lord will be your confidence and will keep your foot from being caught" (Proverbs 3:25-26, NKJV).

Why do we fear our circumstances? How many of those worries ever come true? With so many concerns about the nation and our future, we must place our confidence in God. God says to us in this verse not to fear sudden disaster. Have no fear of the ruin that overtakes the wicked.

The Lord will be our confidence. He is the one who holds our lives in His hands. He will keep your foot from being snared or caught in a trap. There are many opportunities we as humans tend to hold back from doing due to fear. Ask God to remove your fear and replace it with peace. Do not fear what the world fears, for we have an Abba Father, a Daddy God who will be with us and hears our prayers. Step out and try something new.

Daily Requests

- Ask God to give us faith instead of fear and to be our confidence.

- Ask God to speak through you to those in your community, to not fear the uncertainty of this world but rather fear God.

- Pray for the future of the nation that people will put their trust in God rather than the world and its possessions.

Lord, we ask that You replace fear with faith in our lives. We choose to make You our confidence. Be with us and guide us and protect us.

Strong in the Lord

> "Finally, be strong in the Lord and in the power of His might. Put on the full armor of God so that you can take your stand against the devil's schemes (Ephesians 6:10-11).

What does it mean to be strong in the Lord? When we are weak, we go to God for strength. We come before Him in prayer, asking for His help, His guidance, and His direction. We go to God to rest in Him. Do we ever spend time alone with God and listen to Him? If you do not know how to hear the voice of God, ask Him. Ask Him to teach you to hear His voice. God's voice will always draw you toward Him and not push you away.

Do we ever ask God to give us His full armor? Ask Him daily. It is a spiritual armor that enables us to be strong and stand against the devil's schemes.

Also, call each other to pray for each other and for the nation.

Daily Requests

- Ask God to strengthen us in Him and in the power of His might.

- Ask God to open the eyes of believers to the devil's schemes, that we may stand strong against them.

- Pray that people will come to a saving knowledge of the Lord Jesus Christ in your region and nation.

Lord, we ask that You would bring people in our region and nation to a saving knowledge of Jesus Christ. Soften their hearts to You and draw them to You. Do whatever it takes to bring them to salvation.

Exhort One Another

"But exhort one another daily, while it is called 'Today,' lest any of you be hardened through the deceitfulness of sin" (Hebrews 3:13, NKJV).

We are to encourage one another. We are to exhort. What does *exhort* mean? It means to encourage, to urge, and to advise. We are to watch out for one another in a loving manner. We are stronger when we are not alone. How often do we wait until tomorrow to encourage someone?

Is sin deceiving? Isn't that a nature of it? It appears fun. It appears exciting. But in the end, the consequence is death. It is spiritual death and is painful in our lives. God's way brings life.

We are to encourage one another daily. Think of ways to do this *today*.

Daily Requests

- Ask God to teach us to be encouragers.

- Pray that we will be examples to those around us for Him.

- Ask God to change the course of the nation.

God, we ask that You would work in the nation and change the course of it. May Your hand be mighty upon it and bring change. Convict judges to do what is best.

Call to Me

> "Call to me and I will answer you and tell you
> great and unsearchable things you do not know"
> (Jeremiah 33:3).

We've looked at this verse before. This verse is a reminder that God answers when we cry out to Him. Call to Him. Pray to Him. Intercede before Him. Ask Him questions. Seek His advice. Seek His counsel. He says, "I *will* answer you." God answers when we seek Him with all our heart.

Isaiah 50:7 says, "Because the Sovereign Lord helps me, I will not be disgraced. Therefore, I have set my face like flint…"

What does the Lord do? He helps us in our need. We will not be disgraced for seeking Him and His will. His counsel will stand the test. The writer then said, "Therefore…" Therefore what? Therefore, he set his face like flint, because God is judged worthy. Flint is a very hard stone. It is unyielding. Let us set our face and our will firmly to seek the Lord and do His bidding.

What is He asking of you today? What does He want you to do? Take a moment and ask the Lord two requests:

1. Lord God, please show me great and unsearchable secrets that I do not know. (Make this a daily prayer. It will open our eyes of understanding.)

2. What are You, God, asking me to do? Is it small or is it big? (Take a moment to listen.)

Remember that following God will not disgrace you; rather, His blessings follow obedience. Commit your way to the Lord and see if He will not make your way successful.

Daily Requests

- Pray for an understanding of His will to be done.

- Ask God to tell the pastors and Christian leaders in your area great and unsearchable things they do not know.

- Ask God to give supernatural wisdom and insight to leaders in the nation.

Lord, we ask that You reveal Your will to us. Give us creative thoughts and ideas. We call to You and ask that You answer and tell us great and unsearchable things we do not know.

In the Shelter of His Wings

> "Because he loves me, says the Lord, I will rescue him; I will protect him, for he acknowledges my name. He will call upon me, and I will answer him; I will be with him in trouble, I will deliver him and honor him. With long life will I satisfy him and show him my salvation" (Psalms 91:14-16).

Do you remember a situation when God specifically rescued you? What did it feel like? God takes care of us who love Him. David, the psalmist, had many such times that he needed God to step in and rescue him. He was chased by enemies, hid in caves, and lived through many trials and difficulties. Even after he became king, he still, needed God's protection.

"Because he loves me...I will rescue him" (Psalm 91:14). What does it mean to love Him? When we love God, we obey God. Love in action is obedience. Are we perfect? Do we ever fail? Of course! But when we fail, we get back up and walk forward again.

God desires good for us.

Daily Requests

- Pray for love in action in our lives and loved ones.

- Ask God to restore the joy of our salvation.

- Pray for godliness to rise up in our nation and that people will follow and serve God with their whole heart.

Lord, we ask that godliness would rise up in our nation. We ask, that You would increase godliness and lead people to follow and serve You whole heartedly.

To Fear the Lord

"To fear the Lord is to hate evil; I hate pride and arrogance, evil behavior and perverse speech" (Proverbs 8:13).

To fear the Lord is to hate evil.

How often does the culture we live in fear the Lord? To fear the Lord is to respect His wishes. We must know God and His Word to know what He desires. We are to respect Him and act in obedience to Him. So what are God's wishes? God desires that we follow Him in godliness and love. He desires that we flee from evil. He is the opposite of evil. If we love God, we also will hate evil. That is a strong word, to *hate* something. We will love God and what He stands for and abhor evil.

When culture laughs and mocks at evil behavior and perverted speech, we are to abhor it and utterly detest it. We don't support it. What is perverse speech? It is a deliberate deviation from what is normal, good, or holy. We see it on television, in jokes, and even sometimes with coworkers.

Be an example in speech and in conduct. Change the subject quickly or get out of the situation. Stand up for godliness and say you do not care for that kind of talk. Do not laugh at evil.

Daily Requests

- Ask God to help us to be examples and a testimony in our word and in our actions.

- Ask God to draw people around us to godliness that they will be drawn to Christ through our example.

- Ask God to bless and protect Israel and draw the people to salvation.

Lord, we ask that You would work in our lives to enable and encourage us to be Christ-like examples in our words and actions to those around us.

Be Strong and Courageous

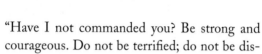

> "Have I not commanded you? Be strong and courageous. Do not be terrified; do not be discouraged, for the Lord your God will be with you wherever you go" (Joshua 1:9).

God commanded Joshua to be strong and courageous. It wasn't a recommendation or an idea; it was a command. God called Joshua to lead and required him to be strong and courageous to do it. On the outside, circumstances may look terrifying, but when we look from God's view, we can see that we are able to do what He calls us to do even when we fear it.

How comforting it is to know that God is with you wherever you go? He says, "I will never leave you nor forsake you" (Hebrews 13:5). That is why we can be courageous in the midst of difficulties or threats. Do you know that God is with you wherever you go?

Do we ever lose our faith in being able to accomplish what we have to do? God told Joshua when he was starting to lead the Israelites to "be strong and courageous." He told him to not be fearful or discouraged because He would be with him wherever he went. God was standing by his side to give him success.

Is there something that God is calling you to do? We are to be obedient. Fear not; it is God who gives enablement.

Daily Requests

- Pray that we will sense God's presence and not be fearful.

- Ask God to draw people to love Him and to love others.

- Ask God to reach into the hearts of those in fear in the nation and give them courage and strength to stand strong in their faith in Him.

Lord, we ask that You would reach into the hearts of people in this nation and by Your Spirit, strengthen them with power in their inner man (Eph. 3:16, NKJV) Break off the lies of the enemy—the devil—and reveal Your truth and love.

The Gift of God's Son

"For unto us a Child is born, unto us a Son is given; and the government will be upon His shoulder. And His name will be called Wonderful Counselor, Mighty God, Everlasting Father, Prince of Peace" (Isaiah 9:6).

Praise God for the miracle of His Son. He is the King of kings and the Lord of lords, and the day will come when every knee shall bow and every tongue confess that Jesus is Lord.

The prophecies said, "O Bethlehem of Judah, you are not just a lowly village in Judah, for a Ruler will come from you who will be the Shepherd for my people Israel'" (Matthew 2).

God took a small village and made it a place where His Son was born. The Lamb of God who takes away the sin of the world was born in the least expected place. What a time and season it was for them to rejoice in the gift that God had given. Remember today the gift that God gave us through His Son, Jesus. When the shepherds heard, they left their flocks to see Jesus. The wise men traveled from far away to give precious gifts to Jesus. What do we have to give Him? Our hearts. Give your heart to God and thank God that He is there in season and out of season.

Daily Requests

- Ask God to be with us, our loved ones, and our families in a special way and to speak to our heart and guide us through the year.

- Pray for those who are lonely and that God will comfort them and surround them with grace.

- Pray for unbelievers in the nation to realize their need for God and turn to Him.

Lord, we ask that Your Spirit would be very real to those who are lonely, that they would feel Your comfort, and that You surround them with Your grace.

The Shepherds

"And there were shepherds living out in the fields nearby, keeping watch over their flocks at night. An angel of the Lord appeared to them, and the glory of the Lord shone around them, and they were terrified" (Luke 2:8-9).

What would it be like to have angels appear to you at night? In the midst of the normal activities, the angel of the Lord appeared to these shepherds. When they least expected, the Savior's birth was announced with the glory of the Lord around them. And they feared. Of all the people to appear to, an angel of the Lord appeared to these shepherds. God does not always appear to those with high status in culture but to those who are normal. And when He did, the shepherds feared.

Have you ever had an encounter with God that frightened you?

"But the angel said to them, 'Do not be afraid. I bring you good news that will cause great joy for all the people...'" (Luke 2:10).

The angel came with good news of the Messiah being born. He came as a baby and laying in a manger in humble circumstances. God shows up in humble times to common people and in common places. The result was that the shepherds returned to praise God.

How often do we thank God for Jesus and for the many blessings we have?

Daily Requests

- Ask God to draw us to Himself and give us an understanding of His ways.

- Pray for people to be touched by the Christmas story and drawn to Christ.

- Ask God to bless, protect, guide, and love the leaders of the nation that they will make right choices.

Lord, we ask for the leaders of the nation, that Your hand will be mighty upon them, and that You will direct them into righteousness.

She Will Give Birth to a Son

"She will give birth to a son, and you are to give him the name Jesus, because he will save his people from their sins. All this took place to fulfill what the Lord had said through the prophet: 'The virgin will be with child and will give birth to a son, and they will call him Immanuel'— which means, 'God with us.' When Joseph woke up, he did what the angel of the Lord had commanded…" (Matthew 1:21-24)

Mary and Joseph must have wondered what this baby would be like—to think that God would conceive a child through His Spirit who would bring salvation to people. To be part of a miracle that God has planned would have to be challenging. Mary and Joseph would be looked at strangely for being pregnant before being married, and the couple's reputations would be looked down upon, certainly.

It would take a lot of trust in God to obey. Yet when Joseph woke up, what did he do? "He did what the angel of the Lord had commanded," and took Mary to be his wife. (Matthew 1:24) That was a risky situation in the human view. He would have to deal with people's gossip. Yet he agreed with God and obeyed.

Do we agree with God and obey, even when it is hard for other people to believe?

Daily Requests

- Ask God to give us faith and courage to stand our ground in the midst of compromise.

- Ask God to speak to people in your neighborhood and draw them to Himself.

- Pray for people in the nation to be drawn to Christ.

Father in heaven, we ask that You speak Your words of truth and love to people throughout the year and draw them to Yourself.

The Birth of Jesus Christ

> "This is how the birth of Jesus Christ came
> about: His mother Mary was pledged to be mar-
> ried to Joseph, but before they came together,
> she was found to be with child through the
> Holy Spirit" (Matthew 1:18).

Mary was a bit younger than girls today that typically get
engaged. Before she and Joseph had any sexual union, she
was discovered to be pregnant. What a surprise for her
husband-to-be.

Because Joseph was a righteous man and did not want
to expose her to public disgrace, so he thought he would
divorce her in private. Obviously, Joseph cared about her
and was righteous (Matthew 1:19), so he also wanted to
protect her. But what a disappointment the pregnancy
must have been.

But after he had considered this, an angel of the Lord
appeared to him in a dream and said, "Joseph son of
David, do not be afraid to take Mary home as your wife,
because what is conceived in her is from the Holy Spirit"
(Matthew 1:20).

What a shock that would be to have an angel of the
Lord appear to you—even in a dream! God's appearance
to Joseph through the dream was dramatic enough to

change his mind and cause him to believe in a miracle. God was on time. He worked through both Mary and Joseph. What a miracle to believe in, even before Jesus was born!

Daily Requests

- Pray for faith in God's calling in your life.

- Pray for unbelief to be removed from the body of Christ and unbelievers to turn to faith in Christ.

- Ask God to pour His mercies upon us, our children, our families, and the nation.

Father in heaven, we ask that You would increase our faith in Your calling in our lives, as well as what You speak into our lives.

In the Lord

"Finally, be strong in the Lord and in his mighty power" (Ephesians 6:10).

We are not so strong on our own. But rather we are strong in the Lord and put on the full armor of God that we can take our stand against the devil's schemes. Be strong and take your stand. What do you know to be a lie? Stand against it. Stand against it with the Word of God. Quote a passage from God's Word. Take a verse and repeat it through the day.

Take the Word of God and repeat it. Use it. Be strong in God's ways. In His path are life and peace. Truth comes through the Word of God. The Spirit of God is also the Spirit of truth, and He imparts truth to us. He illumines our minds and understanding to receive and accept truth that is of God. So ask of God to illumine your heart with truth.

What does God say concerning your situation? What is it that He has to say? Follow Him. Trust Him. He is always right.

Daily Requests

- Ask God to lead you, your family, and loved ones into truth and to illumine your heart with truth.

- Ask God to reveal truth to people in our communities.

- Ask God to illumine the paths of leaders and to guide and direct them into righteousness.

Lord, we ask You to shine Your light and illumine the paths of leaders and to guide and direct them into righteousness. Bring into the light what needs to be brought into Your light and reveal it.

Healing on the Sabbath

"Then he said to the man, 'Stretch out your hand.' So he stretched it out and it was completely restored, just as sound as the other. But the Pharisees went out and plotted how they might kill Jesus" (Matthew 12:13-14).

The Pharisees were looking for an opportunity to accuse Jesus, so they asked if it was lawful to heal on the Sabbath. Jesus cared more about the man being healed than the time it was done. Even the Sabbath was open to do good.

Jesus said to them, "If any of you has a sheep and it falls into a pit on the Sabbath, will you not take hold of it and lift it out? How much more valuable is a man than a sheep…" Then Jesus healed the man right in front of His accusers. Do we care about God and what He cares about, or do we concern ourselves too much with our public appearance? People-pleasing is easy for a time, but it does not reveal the heart of God to others.

Don't worry about what people think of you but instead love each other with a pure heart. Follow God's example and reach out to the poor, the needy, and the less fortunate, and allow God to use you to bring life, healing, and hope in His name.

KARI BITZ

Daily Requests

- Ask God to bring healing where needed in your life.

- Ask God to pour compassion into the lives of Christians to reach out to those who are hurting around them.

- Ask God to reveal Himself in the nation.

Lord, we ask that You bring healing where needed in our lives and in the lives of our loved ones.

We Have a Mighty God

"Confess your trespasses to one another, and pray for one another and that you may be healed. The effective, fervent prayer of a righteous man avails much. Elijah was a man with a nature like ours, and he prayed earnestly that it would not rain; and it did not rain on the land for three years and six months. And he prayed again, and the heaven gave rain, and the earth produced its fruit" (James 5:16-18, NKJV).

God has given us power and ability in prayer. He says, "Call to me, and I will answer you" (Jeremiah 33:3). He is faithful and just. He promises to hear our prayers. What does the first verse say? "The fervent prayer of a righteous man avails much." Be faithful and obedient to God. Confess your sins. God is faithful and just to forgive us and to cleanse us.

Then seek God to know His heart for the situation. Pray with the heart of God. Ask for His heart for situations and relationships you are in. Seek Him on what to pray for. Praying the will of God brings the fruit of the Spirit and His blessings.

Three years is a long time to go without rain, but God used it in His sovereignty to reveal that He was God.

Prayer is powerful. Obedience is also the blessing of God to bring change. When God told Elijah to present himself before King Ahab, Elijah obeyed. God used it to reveal His power and do His will (1 Kings 17-18).

Daily Requests

- Pray that God will give you His heart for prayer and situations around you.

- Ask God to send out workers into the lives of children and to meet their needs and draw them to Christ.

- Ask God to reveal Himself through signs and wonders in the nation.

Lord, we ask that You send out workers into the lives of children. We ask that You direct and enable them to meet the children's needs and draw them to Christ.

Hear and Obey

> "He replied, 'Blessed rather are those who hear the Word of God and obey it'" (Luke 11:28).

Our love for God is revealed by our obedience. Blessed are those who show that they love God by obeying His Word. If we say that we love God but do not obey Him, then do we really love Him? Love and action are the proof. We are to be Jesus's disciples—which means "followers." We imitate Him. We follow Him. This world is passing away, but it is the Word of God that stands forever.

Read the Word of God. Speak it out loud so you also hear it. Hear it. Read it. Dwell on it and obey it. The proof of our love for God is obedience. We choose to witness to non-Christians because God tells us to do so. "Be witnesses" (Acts 1:8, NKJV). His Spirit empowers and enables us to be witnesses.

"But you will receive power when the Holy Spirit comes on you; and you will be my witnesses…" (Acts 1:8).

The first thing that Jesus told His disciples about the Holy Spirit empowering them here is that they would be witnesses for Jesus. "And you will be my witnesses…" We are to raise up the name of Jesus and be obedient to God in it. He calls us to be witnesses for Jesus. Be a witness in your workplace, in your neighborhood, and in the arena of people that God has placed you in. Be a witness. Testify to Jesus. Be obedient and allow His Spirit to lead you and direct you in it.

Daily Requests

- Ask God to open doors of opportunity to share Christ with those around you.

- Ask God to open the eyes of the blind and the ears of the deaf to His Spirit.

- Pray for the poor in the nation to come to an understanding of their need for Jesus and accept Him.

Open my eyes to the people that you desire me to be a witness to and enable me by Your Spirit to be Your witness to them.

Faithful and Wise Servant

> "Who then is the faithful and wise servant, whom the master has put in charge of the servants in his household to give them their food at the proper time? It will be good for that servant whose master finds him doing so when he returns" (Matthew 24:45-46).

God is faithful, and He will reward. This passage first speaks of the fact that we do not know when Jesus will return. It says no one knows the day or hour of His return. Only the Father knows. Therefore, because we do not know when Jesus will return, we are to be faithful and wise. We are to keep watch and be ready because He will return at an hour when we do not expect Him to.

Therefore, be wise. What is wisdom? It is knowledge that is applied. Do you know what God's calling is in your life? Be faithful to obey. If you do not know, then look at the Word of God. Be faithful where you are with what you have been given. Feed the poor, help the sick, love one another, and love God first. Make the time to serve and give of your money, time, and resources, for we do not know when He will return and reward the faithful and wise.

Be faithful. Continue to persevere in the will of God. Do not give up hope. Do not give up patience, for there is a reward coming. Be faithful, for we do not know when He is coming.

Daily Requests

- Ask God to renew your hope, perseverance, and commitment to His will for you.

- Pray for the needy and the poor to be supplied for.

- Ask God to send the workers into the harvest fields of the needy in the nation and that they will be helped and drawn to Christ.

Lord, we ask that Your people would see the needs of the poor and needy and reach out to help them.

Joseph's Success

"The Lord was with Joseph and he prospered, and he lived in the house of his Egyptian master. When his master saw that the Lord was with him and that the Lord gave him success in everything he did, Joseph found favor in his eyes and became his attendant…" (Genesis 39:2-4).

Joseph was betrayed by his own brothers, thrown into a well, and sold into slavery. Then an Egyptian, who was one of the Pharaoh's officials, bought him and took him to live in his house as his slave. What happened then? His master saw that the Lord was with him and that the Lord gave him success in everything he did.

So his master gave him a promotion, and he was placed in charge of Pharaoh's household to care for everything the Pharaoh owned. Pharaoh's whole household was blessed. Joseph could have moped that he had been betrayed and could have decided not to work as hard. He could have sat in bitterness about his hardships, but he worked hard and was promoted.

The Lord was still with him in the middle of his hardships. God is with us even when we hurt. Turn to the Lord and work hard wherever you are. In the midst of it is an opportunity for blessing if you remain with the Lord and remain with those He has called you to remain with.

Daily Requests

- Ask God for wisdom and guidance to be faithful in the midst of difficult circumstances.

- Ask God to bless His servants with patience and endurance and hope that God will reward His servants as they continue.

- Ask God to change the hearts of the leadership in the nation to love Him and follow godliness.

- Ask God to bless Israel and draw them to Christ.

Lord, we ask that you change the hearts of those in leadership in the nation and to love You and follow godliness.

Lift Up Hands in Prayer

> "I want men everywhere to lift up holy hands in prayer, without anger or disputing" (1 Timothy 2:8).

Before this, starting in verse 1, Timothy encourages that we pray, request, and intercede and give thanks for everyone. He specifically mentions kings and all those in authority that we may live godly and peaceful lives. We must pray for the leaders in the nation, in our region, and in the community or church that is our own.

Then, if you have ever doubted that you can lift up your hands in prayer, the apostle Paul says it all. Men everywhere are encouraged to lift up holy hands in prayer. We are to be united in prayer rather than in anger. We are also to be public about our love for God and our worship of God. We are not to hide our worship of God. Lift up your hands to God and let them be holy hands set aside for Him in purity and devotion to God.

Do we have anger between us? Is there a brother or sister in Christ that you have anger against? Go to them and do whatever you are able to do to make peace with them. Apologize and forgive. Do your part. Let go of your disagreements with others. Rather, love one another and pray with faith, knowing that your prayers are not hindered by un-forgiveness. Lift your hands in prayer and worship God publicly.

Daily Requests

- Ask God to create in us a pure heart.

- Ask God to lead His people to pray always and to lift their hands in prayer and worship without anger or disputing.

- Ask God to give us courage to share our faith with others in the nation, until we each shine God's light in our region.

Lord, we ask that You create in us a pure heart that is cleansed, renewed, and revived for Your glory.

Work Heartily with Confidence

> "Whatever you do, work at it with all your heart, as working for the Lord, not for men, since you know that you will receive an inheritance from the Lord as a reward" (Colossians 3:23-24).

If you want a raise or a promotion, the first thing to do is to work heartily as unto the Lord. Do more than you are required, and eventually you will be promoted. Work with a good attitude and with your heart. Keep in mind that it is the Lord that you are serving, and He is willing to reward you. He has good things in store.

Do not be concerned about the attitudes of others but rather shine in your area of expertise. Look at your work as a service. Serve heartily and with passion, and it is God who will reward you. And, in principle, it is the people who work hard that tend to come upon success. The verse says, "whatever you do." Whether you are washing windows for a living or are a bank clerk or in a managerial position, God is with you and desires that you work at it as unto Him, for it is He who will reward you.

What would you do differently if God was standing by your side watching you? If it is difficult to have a good attitude and love God in your work, begin by asking

Him to help you in it. Daily, ask God to give you His thoughts toward it and increase your love for God even in your work. Ask and you shall receive (Matthew 7:7).

Daily Requests

- Ask God to give you His thoughts toward your work at home or at the job.

- Pray for God to reveal Himself to believers and pour out His Spirit upon us.

- Ask God to change the heart of the nation and bring truth, love, and fruitfulness.

Lord, we ask that You change the heart of the nation and bring truth, love, and fruitfulness through Your Spirit.

The Spirit of Truth

> "But when he, the Spirit of truth comes, He will guide you into all truth. He will not speak on His own; He will speak only what He hears, and He will tell you what is yet to come" (John 16:13).

When Jesus went to heaven, He sent the Holy Spirit who is the Spirit of truth. He is the one who gives us understanding. It is through Him that we can understand truth. He guides us into truth.

If we do not know Christ, we do not have the Spirit of God living and working in us. Those who do not have a personal relationship with Christ do not have the Spirit of truth. It is through God's Spirit that the eyes of our understanding are opened to Christ and to the knowledge of Him. After we know Christ, we have access to the mind of Christ that comes through the Holy Spirit.

The Holy Spirit guides us into truth.

If there are situations in your life and relationships that you do not currently understand, ask God to reveal truth. What is the offense? What is the issue? What is the timing? What is the revelation and understanding from the Holy Spirit that comes? Ask and wait upon the Lord. Continue to ask.

Daily Requests

- Ask God to guide His people into truth and our families to live in the knowledge of Him.

- Pray for God's truth to dwell and simmer in our communities to bring freedom, healing, and strength.

- Pray that God will cause godly people and principles to rise up in this nation and make a difference for Christ.

Lord, we ask that Your truth will dwell and take root in our communities and that You bring freedom, healing, and strength through it.

Richly Rewarded

"So do not throw away your confidence; it will be richly rewarded" (Hebrews 10:35).

We all have seasons where we become discouraged, but the Word of God tells us to keep our confidence, for it will be richly rewarded. Why do we not give up? We will be richly rewarded for persevering. It's not just rewarded; rather, it is *richly* rewarded.

There is no substitute for God's rewards. The rewards that He gives are blessings beyond what we can find on our own. He knows the past and the present and is fully aware of what is coming down the road.

Our confidence, our full assurance, is placed in God and what He has for us. He has a reward if we continue. Do not give up! God is good. We may not see the reward, but we believe. The reward will come, and it is a good reward.

Daily Requests

- Ask God to increase our confidence in Him, His Word, and His principles.

- Ask God to reveal Himself in a new way to non-Christians.

- Pray for Israel and that God will both protect and strengthen them.

Father in heaven, we ask that You will protect and strengthen Israel. Bring people to You.

One in Christ

> "And the glory which You gave Me I have given them and that they may be one just as We are one" (John 14:22).

How will we as the body of Christ be one just as God and Christ are one? Is there any way except through love? In the verse above, Jesus prayed for unity amongst Christians. The apostle Paul also prayed for this amongst Christians:

> "That Christ may dwell in your hearts through faith; that you, being rooted and grounded in love, may be able to comprehend with all the saints what is the width and length and depth and height to know the love of Christ which passes knowledge" (Ephesians 3:17-19a).

We must put on love and be rooted, grounded, and established in it. That sounds like a foundation. Love must be in, around, and through, our relationships. Then we will be able to understand, in unity with other believers, the greatness of Christ's love, "which passes knowledge."

Jesus prayed that we as Christians would be one just as the Father and the Son are one. We must grow in our relationships with one another. We are all a part of the body.

Each part should resemble God in one way or another. We have differences and distinctions, and yet we unite in our love for Christ. We love and accept one another and grow up in Christ as part of the body of Christ.

We, as believers, shine God's love to a world that does not know Him through the way that we treat each other. People will be drawn to Christ through our unity and love.

Daily Requests

- Ask God to encourage your heart and teach us to love one another just as He loves us.

- Pray that God will bring people to great hope with a saving knowledge of the Lord Jesus Christ.

- Pray that God will raise up righteousness in the nation.

Lord, we ask that You will work to raise up righteousness and godly standards in the nation. Convict leaders as needed and reveal the greatness of Your love and ways.

Except by Prayer and Fasting

> "Then the disciples came to Jesus in private and asked, 'Why couldn't we drive it out?' He replied, 'Because you have so little faith. I tell you the truth, if you have faith as small as a mustard seed, you can say to this mountain, "Move from here to there" and it will move. Nothing will be impossible for you. But this kind does not go out except by prayer and fasting'" (Matthew 17:19-21, KJV).

What does Jesus link together? In verse 20, He speaks of faith being the qualifier or the ability that accomplishes what was impossible without it. Then the verse right after says it also depends on prayer and fasting. Why does our culture in this day and age ignore fasting? Why are so many of us, as Christians, not interested in fasting? How is it related to our culture and the feel good desire that we have? Our culture wants what feels good *now*.

Yet there is power and ability that comes through fasting and prayer. I remember hearing of a lady who got excited when she had hunger pains from fasting because she knew that strongholds were being torn down. That is exciting! That is faith in action.

Fasting and prayer increases our ability to see beyond our need and reach out to others. It also increases our need for God. Many people find it increases their faith, as well. There are some situations that need the mighty hand of God to prevail. Sometimes we need a miracle. Fasting and prayer is the next step in seeking God earnestly.

Daily Requests

- Ask God to increase fasting and prayer in the nation.

- Pray that our families would have blinders removed and strongholds broken.

- Pray for our nation to be humbled before God and to come before Him in unity and repentance for a new day to dawn.

Lord, we ask that You would increase fasting and prayer in the nation. Speak to the hearts of leaders and people in the nation to seek You in prayer and fasting.

Hope is Good

"Hope deferred makes the heart sick, but when the desire comes, it is a tree of life" (Proverbs 13:12, NKJV).

Time can take a toll on the heart when longings and hopes are not fulfilled. It can be difficult to wait for your children to come to Christ. It can be hard to continue to pray for concerns that you don't see quick answers to, but know that God is at work.

He hears your prayers and has a way of fulfilling them. You don't see the results as quickly as painting a house, necessarily, but that is because work on the inside of man is often time consuming. God is patient and understands the heart of man. He knows our children's hearts perfectly. Allow Him to continue His work and continue to hope.

Daily Requests

- Ask God to bring the prodigals back to Him in our families and loved ones.

- Pray for hearts of understanding with people we know.

- Pray that God will cause godly people and principles to rise up in this nation and make a difference for Christ.

Lord, we ask that You would give us hearts of understanding with the people around us and that we can have the ability to pray with insight and reach out with hope.

Prayer for Love to Abound

"I pray that your love may abound more and more in all knowledge and depth of insight..." (Philippians 1:9).

Does knowledge make a difference in our lives? How does it help to know more about a person and his situation? God knows each one of us from the inside out. He knows our comings and our goings, our shortcomings, and our struggles. He understands our deepest thoughts and emotions and cares for us.

So the apostle Paul prays that the Philippians' love will increase in knowledge and depth of insight. God is the one who can give you understanding. Ask for it. The next verse reads this way:

"...so that you may be able to discern what is best and may be pure and blameless until the day of Christ" (Philippians 1:10).

What is the second part of the prayer? It is that you may be able to know or distinguish what is best and may be pure and blameless (righteous) until the day of Christ. We will be able to respond and act rightly.

Is there a relationship or are there a few relationships that you need love to abound in knowledge and depth of insight? Pray this verse for these and watch how God answers your prayers.

Daily Requests

- Ask God to cause our love to abound more and more in all knowledge and depth of insight.

- Ask God to give us love and knowledge with insight in our relationships with those who don't know Christ yet (coworkers, neighbors, etc.).

- Pray for God to bring spiritual awakening to our nation, to pour out His Spirit upon us, and to bring change for His glory.

Lord, we ask that You pour out Your Spirit upon us and bring awakening, refreshing, and revival to our nation. Change the hearts of man for Your glory.

To Serve

"Jesus knew that the Father had put all things under His power, and that He had come from God and was returning to God; so He got up from the meal and took off His outer clothing, and wrapped a towel around His waist. After that, He poured water into a basin and began to wash His disciples' feet, drying them with the towel that was wrapped around Him" (John 13:3-5).

Jesus knew that the Father God put all things under His power. He knew where He came from and where He was going. He was God's Son, a title with prestige and power. Then it says, "so..." Because of this, Jesus got up and became a servant to His disciples as an example to us. How many places in our world do prestige and power meld with humility and servant-hood? Human nature tends toward pride or arrogance. The worldly ways tend to want to be served rather than serve others.

Yet Jesus knew He had great authority and power. And He was God's only Son—fully human and fully God. "So" He laid it all on the line to be a servant to His disciples. How often do we lay it on the line to serve our brothers and sisters in Christ? How often do we forgo our human nature and worldly ways to humble ourselves and serve others to meet their needs? Yet service is one of the most fun and fulfilling things we can do. It is in service that our own needs are often met, as well. God has a way of rewarding us for our humility and obedience.

Daily Requests

- Ask God to open your eyes for opportunities to serve as Christ did.

- Ask God to open the eyes of believers to realize that some of our most fulfilling times are in service to Him.

- Ask God to cause the leadership in our nation to be servant leaders and service-minded for the sake of the kingdom.

Lord, we ask that You open our eyes for opportunities to serve as Jesus did.

Do Not Worry!

> "Therefore I tell you, do not worry about your life, what you will eat or drink; or about your body, what you will wear. Is not life more important than food, and the body more important than clothes?" (Matthew 6:25).

What issues concern you most? What do you think about and place your focus on the most? Is it possessions? Is it temporal? Do we concern ourselves with having enough?

Jesus said, "Do not worry about your life, what you will eat or drink; or about your body, what you will wear." Do not worry about it. Do not fret about it. Jesus goes on to say in verse 33, "But seek first His kingdom and His righteousness, and all these things will be given to you as well." How often we stuff our homes and lives with possessions our world considers important. It wears out. It runs out and grows old. But the fulfillment and peace which God gives is lasting. He knows that we have physical needs. The principle is to place God first, set our eyes on Him, and do His will.

Daily Requests

- Pray that you and your family will seek first His kingdom and His righteousness Ask God to clarify what is important.

- Ask God to set people free from lies that hold them back from healing.

- Pray that God will bring salvation to our nation and cause righteousness to rise up for His glory!

Lord, we ask that You set people free from lies that stop them from healing. Reveal truth in love to them.

The God of Hope

"So I pray that God, who gives you hope, will
keep you happy and full of peace as you believe
in Him. May you overflow with hope through
the power of Holy Spirit" (Romans 15:13, NLT).

Have you ever prayed this prayer for your family and yourself? It is amazing the result that comes with it. Regardless
of the situation, we can hope in God. Hope here comes
through the power of the Holy Spirit. He is the God who
is faithful and is able to fulfill His promises to His people.

What is the condition to our being filled with His joy
and peace? It often includes two things. The first here is
that he prayed for it. He asked God to fill them with all
joy and peace as they trust in Him. The second part we
see is that they choose to trust in Him as the God of hope.
We choose to place our trust in Him. It is active.

What is God asking you to do today?

Daily Requests

- Ask God to fill you and your family and loved ones
  with all joy and peace in believing and that you may
  abound in hope—be filled with hope—by the power
  of the Holy Spirit.

KARI BITZ

- Pray that God will bring restoration of godly principles in this nation.

- Ask God to protect and strengthen Israel.

Lord, we ask that You restore godly principles in the nation and that people will see the good fruit that they lead to and follow You.

Washed Seven Times

> "Now Naaman was commander of the army
> of the king of Aman. He was a great man in
> the sight of his master and highly regarded,
> because through him the Lord had given vic-
> tory to Aram. He was a valiant soldier, but he
> had leprosy… [Naaman was sent to Israel to
> be healed.] …So Naaman went with his horses
> and chariots and stopped at the door of Elisha's
> house. Elisha sent a messenger to say to him,
> 'Go, wash yourself seven times in the Jordan,
> and your flesh will be restored and you will be
> cleansed'" (2 Kings 5:1, 9-10).

Healing is often a process. Naaman needed to humble
himself first to seek help. Then he needed to humble
himself from his high position to be willing to do what
a prophet of God told him to do. Then he needed to be
willing to do it repeatedly to receive healing. Often this is
also what God requires of us. He asks us to ask for help.
Then we are required to lay down our need for self-suffi-
ciently and be humble enough to do what is asked of us. It
is often a process that may take many repetitions to bring
about. It is God who heals, but it requires obedience. The
story continues:

"So he [Naaman] went down and dipped himself in the Jordan seven times, as the man of God had told him, and his flesh was restored and became clean like that of a young boy" (2 Kings 5:14).

Obedience brought healing. Where there are areas that you need healing, continue to seek God. Then be obedient.

Daily Requests

- Ask God to bring healing where needed in our families and loved ones.

- Pray that God will manifest His presence in our churches and bring healing in relationships.

- Ask God to bring repentance in the nation that people will turn to make Him Lord and Savior in their lives.

- Ask God to strengthen and protect Israel!

Lord, we ask that You bring healing to every place that is needed in our families and loves ones. Heal us and restore us.

He Reached Down

"He reached down from on high and took hold of me; he drew me out of deep waters. He rescued me from the powerful enemy, from my foes, who were strong for me" (2 Samuel 22:17-18).

David sang this song to the Lord after the Lord delivered him from the hand of all his enemies. He had several years of being chased by his enemies before becoming king. But God was his support. God is our support. He is with us as we remain with Him. He is with us even when we leave, but when we leave, we are not dwelling under His shelter or protection and can be hurt by sin.

God is our God. He is faithful to the end. If you have had times that have been difficult to walk through and stay strong with God, keep your head up. Stay close to the Father in heaven who knows your need. Pour out your heart to Him and draw close. Allow others to strengthen you, as well. Do not be a hermit. Even David had people around him.

Trust in the Lord and He will make your righteousness shine. He will be your lamp by your side to enlighten the step ahead of you. Allow Him to guide you in the ways that are best.

Daily Requests

- Ask God to deliver you and strengthen you.

- Pray for the body of Christ to draw near to God.

- Ask God to speak to the hearts of people in the nation and to convict them of what is right and wrong.

Lord, we ask that You speak to the hearts of people in the nation. Open their eyes to realize their need for you and convict them of what is right and wrong.

Our God of Hope

"Trust in the Lord with all your heart and lean not on your own understanding; in all your ways acknowledge him, and he will make your paths straight" (Proverbs 3:5-6).

Do you ever feel a little odd when you are following God? Some people think we must act like the world, talk like the world, and walk as the world—but God has called us to a higher way. It is a way of depending, trusting and hoping in Him, in His ways, and in His will.

His plans are perfect. We, as humans, mess up at times. But God is there to hold us and to provide a way out of our mess if we will turn to Him to lean on Him. He is a compassionate father, our daddy God (Mark 14:36), and we can turn to Him even when we fail. Trust in the Lord with all your heart. Lean on Him. Lean on His ways and His understanding.

He has a plan. He has a mission. He will bring you to it, and His promise is this: He will make your paths straight. In all your ways, acknowledge Him, and He shall direct your paths (Proverbs 3:6, NKJV).

Trust in the Lord daily.

Daily Requests

- Ask God to counsel you in the way to go.

- Ask God to counsel His people in His ways and plans and that they will be open hearted to Him.

- Ask God to increase righteousness in the nation and to destroy the plans of the wicked.

Lord, we ask that You counsel Your people in Your ways and plans. Open our hearts to You so that we will be responsive, obedient, and in love with You.

The True Light

"All things were made through Him, and without Him nothing was made that was made. In Him was life, and the life was the light of men. And the light shines in the darkness, and the darkness did not comprehend it" (John 1:3-5, NKJV).

Do you know people who do not understand the love of God in Christ? The darkness does not understand. The world does not realize their need for Christ because the god of this age has blinded their eyes. Spiritual truth is not understandable to the natural man until the Holy Spirit comes to illumine our hearts and minds.

Have you ever walked in a dark room and tried to find something? It is difficult in the dark. Sometimes we don't find what we're looking for, especially if it is not where we thought it was. People need the Lord. They have spiritual darkness without the Holy Spirit and the light of His people reaching out. We are to be examples of God's love and truth in other people's lives. As a city set on a hill, shining the light of Christ, so are we to shine God's love and truth into the lives of people around us.

In Christ is life. It is the abundant and purposeful life that God has called us to. In this life, He calls us to reach out to those who are living in darkness and do not understand Him. And in this calling to reach out and shine His light forth we find blessings.

Daily Requests

- Ask God to give you creative ways to reach out to those around you.

- Ask God to shine His light and truth through His people into the darkness so that people will be drawn to Him.

- Pray for the Holy Spirit to convict the world of sin and righteousness, as needed (John 16:8).

Lord, we ask that Your precious Spirit would convict the world of sin and righteousness as needed. We ask that Your Spirit would open people's eyes to realize truth in the nation. We need You.

Born of God

> "But as many as received Him and to them He gave the right to become children of God and to those who believe in His name: who were born, not of blood, nor of the will of the flesh, nor of the will of man, but of God" (John 1:12-13, NKJV).

What must we do to be children of God? First we receive Him and believe in His name. Whose name do we believe in? We believe in Jesus. He is the Word. Believe in the Lord Jesus, and you will be saved.

We believe that Jesus is the name above every name. He is the Savior of the world and the light that illumines people's lives to truth. We are not born by natural ways with flesh and blood into the family of God; rather, we come to be children of God through our faith and acceptance of Jesus, God's Son, and His payment for our sins on the cross.

So we are children of God. He is our father, and we have access to Him through prayer. When we pray, He hears and answers. He loves us. He guides us and protects us.

Daily Requests

- Ask God to reveal Himself to us as our Father.

- Ask God to speak truth in love into the lives and hearts of men.

- Ask God to soften the hearts of the lost in the nation and provide Christians in their lives.

Lord, we ask for Your grace and truth in our lives. Reveal Your love and faithfulness. Speak truth in love into the lives and hearts of men.

Keep a Clear Conscience

> "And I have the same hope in God as these men and that there will be a resurrection of both the righteous and the wicked. So I strive always to keep my conscience clear before God and man" (Acts 24:15).

We are judged for our actions by God when we are raised up. Did we follow Him? Did we obey His call? Paul strived to please God and to keep his conscience clear before God and man. He kept himself from sin.

Remember that the life we live will bring rewards for eternity as we live for God. He rewards His children for obedience. Our obedience here will surely bring blessings and rewards from God. He rewards those who are faithful to continue in His Word and be led by His Spirit.

What is God calling you to do today? Read your Bible daily. Pray. Ask God to teach you, lead you and fill you with His Spirit.

Daily Requests

- Ask God to guide you in His ways and His truth and to be led by His Spirit.

- Ask God to open the hearts of Christians to the desire of God to love people unselfishly.

- Pray for the leaders of the nation to be convicted of sin as needed and come to repentance.

Lord, we ask that leaders of the nation would be convicted of sin as needed. Bring them to repentance to place You first and keep You first in their lives.

Jesus Went by Himself to Pray

"Immediately Jesus made the disciples get into the boat and go on ahead of him to the other side, while he dismissed the crowd" (Matthew 14:22-23).

After He had dismissed them, He went up on a mountainside by Himself to pray. When evening came, He was there alone.

Jesus had just fed five thousand men plus women and children off of five loaves of bread and two fish. Immediately, Jesus sent the disciples off in the boat, dismissed the crowd of people who were happily satisfied from the food, and went by Himself up on a mountainside to pray.

After a busy time with others around, Jesus set aside time to spend in the presence of the Father. He made it a priority to spend time with God the Father. How often the temptation is to spend less time with God when our schedules are busy. Jesus made the time. He even sent the disciples off ahead of him.

There are times that it is healthy for you to have a time of rest. Rest in the Lord. Be of good courage, and He shall strengthen your heart.

Wait on the Lord, be of good courage, and He shall strengthen your heart.

Daily Requests

- Ask the Lord for His blessing and love.

- Pray that the body of Christ will unite in prayer more and more.

- Ask God to open the eyes of understanding of people in the nation to know and realize truth.

Lord, we ask that You would bless us, reach into our need, and meet us where we are. We ask for Your love to abound in our lives and that we will know the greatness of Your love for us and respond to it.

Compelled by the Love of Christ

"If we are out of our mind, it is for the sake of God; if we are in our right mind, it is for you. For Christ's love compels us, because we are convinced that one died for all, and therefore all died. And he died for all and that those who live should no longer live for themselves but for him who died for them and was raised again" (2 Corinthians 5:13-15).

Have you ever had people consider you out of your mind for God? Have they thought you were weird to rather go on a mission trip than on a cruise? They thought the same of Jesus. Paul says here that it is Christ's love that compels them. They cannot stop from sharing their faith with others. They try to persuade men.

As Christians we are convinced that Christ died for all. So those who live, live in Christ. Our life is now hidden together with Christ. It is no longer for our own benefit and pleasing that we live. We live to serve Christ. Do you know that your greatest joy will be in serving God? It is in living for God vibrantly and passionately that we find what we are looking for. Our souls are filled with the grace of God.

Christ died for all. He loved us that much. He died for all that we should no longer live for ourselves. Live for God.

Daily Requests

- Ask God to encourage our hearts in Him.

- Ask God to bless families in the nation and enable them to shine for God.

- Pray for the angels of God to protect His leaders in the nation.

Lord, we ask that You will bless the families in the nation and shine through them. Reach in to their need and meet them where they are.

Do Not Be Drunk with Wine

"And do not be drunk with wine, in which is dissipation; but be filled with the Spirit" (Ephesians 5:18, NKJV).

When you look at people who drink, does it look fun? Look at the lives of those who continue to drink and at what drunk people look like. It is a way to avoid issues, but it is not a way to heal and overcome them. It is only avoidance. God says to "be filled with the Spirit." The Holy Spirit gives us a lasting joy and fulfillment.

What is dissipation? It is a reference to wasting something by misuse. It is an extreme pursuit of pleasure but is something that can waste our gifts and abilities. God desires good for us. His plans are for good. Be filled with the Spirit of God who loves you and brings into your life blessings as you follow the Him. It is the Spirit of God who brings life and fulfillment and joy.

The consequences of sin are often more sin. Sin breeds sin. Righteousness brings more righteousness. Where the Spirit of the Lord is there is freedom.

Daily Requests

- Ask God to pour truth into your hearts.

- Pray for the lost to come to salvation and to receive the gift of salvation in Christ.

- Ask God to raise up godly leaders in the churches in our region.

Lord, we ask that You would raise up godly leaders. Ordain them. Work through them and give them courage and faith to lead willingly and graciously.

Don't Be Afraid

"During the fourth watch of the night Jesus went out to them, walking on the lake. When the disciples saw him walking on the lake, they were terrified. 'It's a ghost,' they said, and cried out in fear. But Jesus immediately said to them: 'Take courage! It is I. Don't be afraid'" (Matthew 14:25-27).

What would you think if you saw someone walking on the water? The disciples were in the boat on the lake buffeted by waves and wind when they saw Jesus walking on the water, but they didn't recognize Him at first.

The first words Jesus spoke were, "Take courage! It is I. Don't be afraid." Do not be afraid when things go awry. Do not fear when things go differently than you expect. God is with you in the storms. He is near you when you draw near to Him.

Why does the Word speak so frequently about not fearing? The more we obey God, the less we have to fear. The consequences of obedience are blessings. We avoid evil by obeying. We avoid pitfalls and traps of the devil when we follow Christ. I choose Christ.

Daily Requests

- Ask God to guard us from temptation.

- Ask God to draw people near to Him and to speak to them in the watches of the night when they are open to hearing.

- Ask God to open the eyes of understanding of people in the nation to truth and bring conviction of sin when needed.

Lord, we ask that You protect us from evil and guard us from temptation. We ask You to bring Your Word to our hearts and minds and speak. Keep us from sin.

God Answers Prayer

"Call to me and I will answer you and tell you great and unsearchable things you do not know" (Jeremiah 33:3).

The Spirit of God reveals the hidden things of God to us. It is by His Spirit, His presence, and His truth that we see accurately and understand rightly. The precious Spirit gives us understanding of that which we could never understand on our own. "Call to me," says the Lord, "and I will answer you and tell you things that you do not understand." Take time today to ask the Lord to teach you and give you understanding.

The only way for people to understand who God is, is through His body and through revelation of His Word and Spirit. It is the Spirit of God that opens the eyes of understanding that only He can open. What God speaks to you may be different from the message that He gives to someone else because He is a personal God and knows your needs.

Ask God also to open your heart to receive and trust what He has for you. You can even ask Him for a confirmation of it. If it is a decision-making word, ask a friend (or friends) to pray about it for you as well to confirm it.

Daily Requests

- Ask God to tell us great and unsearchable things we do not know. Ask Him for confirmation, if needed.

- Pray for the body of Christ to rise up in faith and understanding.

- Ask God to forgive the sins of our nation and have mercy upon us.

Lord, we ask that You forgive the sins of our nation. Forgive pride and arrogance. We ask for Your mercy and forgiveness.

The Lord's Ways

"'For my thoughts are not your thoughts, neither are your ways my ways,' declares the Lord. 'As the heavens are higher than the earth, so are my ways higher than your ways and my thoughts than your thoughts'" (Isaiah 55:8).

Have you ever had a time when you wondered, "God, what are you doing?" And yet, He sees perfectly. It is not always His actions that have brought things about but rather the sins and disobedience of His children or other people. God's ways are not our ways. There are times, inevitably, and seasons that we do not understand what God is doing, but with obedience and faith comes understanding.

How often do we want proof before we will start a venture or step out in obedience to God? Are there times when you wait too long and lag behind the will of God because of your concern for your needs being met? Here is the assurance that we have. He is able to supply. If you are in the will of God, count on Him supplying your needs. Act in faith and step out in obedience. Begin the process and allow God to open doors to amply supply for your needs. Ask Him to provide.

There will always be provision in the will of God. Follow God.

Daily Requests

- Ask God for faith to step out into the ventures that He wills for us.

- Ask God for His love to fill up and overflow from His body to the needy around us.

- Pray for the lost to come to salvation and for leaders to follow godliness and walk in His ways.

Lord, we ask that You renew and revive our faith. Give us increased faith and Your word in mind and heart to step into the ventures that You will for us. Give us courage and faith to obey.

By Faith in Christ

"This righteousness from God comes through faith in Jesus Christ to all who believe. There is no difference, for all have sinned and fall short of the glory of God, and are justified freely by His grace through the redemption that came by Christ Jesus" (Romans 3:22-24).

We are made in right standing with God through our faith in Christ. Faith that is active has actions with it, but it is not actions that cause us to be righteous. It is faith first. Every person falls short of God's glory. But God, who is rich in mercy, has made a way where there was no way previously for us to come to Him redeemed and justified and righteous.

What does it mean to be redeemed? It speaks of God delivering us from sin. He saved us from what we could not save ourselves from. We are either slaves to sin, or we choose to be bondservants of God and righteousness. Without God, we are unable to deliver ourselves. But God, who is rich in mercy, has provided us with His Son and the free gift of salvation to all who receive Him. Praise God! With God, all things are possible.

We walk by faith in Christ. We are not of this world. Rather, we have been born into a new life and justified by Christ. We are Christ's followers, and so we walk by faith.

Daily Requests

- Ask God to open our eyes to see His hand guiding us.

- Ask God to open the eyes of the church to receive His gifts and calling.

- Ask God to bring repentance in the nation so that people will realize their need for Christ.

Lord, we ask that You open the eyes of believers in the church and for us to receive Your gifts, recognize Your gifts, and walk in Your calling for each of us. Help us to realize that our greatest fulfillment is in following You.

Ask God to Lead and Guide

> "Turn your ear to me, come quickly to my rescue;
> be my rock of refuge, a strong fortress to save me.
> Since you are my rock and my fortress, for the sake
> of your name lead and guide me" (Psalms 31:2-3).

David appeals to God to rescue Him and to lead and guide for His name's sake. Do we pray for God's glory to be revealed when we pray? Do we ask God to change the hearts of people in our nation for His glory and honor? It is the glory of God to conceal a matter and the glory of kings to search it out. Another translation says, "It is God's privilege to conceal things and the king's privilege to discover them" (Proverbs 25:1, NLT).

There is a dependency upon God that is expressed in this prayer. Though at times we can do all we can, it is in God's counsel, His power, and answer to our prayer that times can change. We may know some of what to do according to our natural mind, but it is the mind of God that knows best. His Spirit reveals truth and ways in situations that we cannot know on our own.

Appeal to God on the basis of His name and for His glory. How will it bring glory to God? Ask Him to do it (lead and guide you). Because we are God's children, we have access to Him.

Daily Requests

- Ask God to lead and guide you for the sake of His name and for His glory.

- Pray for the lost to come to salvation because He loves them so much.

- Ask Him to change the heart of the nation for the glory of His name.

Lord, we ask that You change the heart of the nation for the glory of Your name. We ask that You would glorify Christ in the nation, soften the hearts of unbelievers, and draw them to You.

New Hope

"Very early on the first day of the week, just after sunrise, they were on their way to the tomb and they asked each other, 'Who will roll the stone away from the entrance of the tomb?'" (Mark 16:2-3).

Have you ever noticed that the three women here thought about the stone being too large for them to roll away only after they were already on their way? But when they got to the tomb, they saw that the stone had already been moved. Rather than what they expected to find in the tomb, they soon were told by an angel that Jesus was alive. How could that be? They had not understood what was to come that Jesus would be raised from the dead and overcome death and hell. It had never happened before.

But now God had moved the stone away and had given them the great news that Jesus was alive. "Trembling and bewildered, the women went out and fled from the tomb" (verse 8). Would you be shocked? What would you do?

After Jesus suffered the worst death imaginable, God healed him and raised Him up. God is able to do the unimaginable—a miracle. For we have been brought into a new hope—a *living* hope—through the resurrection of Jesus Christ from the dead (1 Peter 1:3). What can be the worst of circumstances can actually be turned into a living hope by God if we stay with Him and decide to follow Jesus.

Take the difficult hurts in your life and allow God to turn them around for good.

Daily Requests

- Ask God to guide you and direct you in His ways.

- Pray for the love of God to fill up the body of Christ and to overflow into the lives of people.

- Ask God to soften the hearts of the lost to Him and His ways and to bring spiritual awakening in the nation.

Lord, we ask that You would take the difficulties that have been in our lives and turn them for good. Guide us and direct us in Your ways.

Fear Not

> "Jesus was in the stern, sleeping on a cush-
> ion. The disciples woke him and said to him,
> 'Teacher, don't you care if we drown?' He got
> up, rebuked the wind and said to the waves,
> 'Quiet! Be still!' Then the wind died down and
> it was completely calm. He said to his disciples,
> 'Why are you so afraid? Do you still have no
> faith?' (Mark 4:38-40).

Do you have faith in God? The disciples had taken Jesus
in the boat with them to cross the lake. A "furious squall"
developed and threatened to overwhelm or swamp the
boat (Mark 4:37). Jesus was sleeping through it, but the
disciples were overcome with worry. They were afraid
of drowning, even though Jesus was there.

He got up, rebuked the wind, and commanded the
waves to "be still," (Mark 4:39) and they obeyed him.
Imagine seeing Jesus rebuke the wind and the waves.
Allow Jesus to calm the wind and the waves in your life.
Do not fear drowning in difficulties. Keep people around
you who love God and who are there for you when you
need them. Love God and love one another.

To feel fear is normal, but how we react to it is the
determining factor. Do not allow yourself to be controlled

by your feelings. Have faith in God and go to the people that God has placed around you. Look for godly counsel.

Daily Requests

- Ask God for His peace that passes all understanding and His godly counsel in your life and loved ones' lives.

- Pray for those who do not know Christ to see the example of Christ in our lives as we follow Him.

- Pray for the leadership in the nation to listen to godly counsel.

Lord, we ask that You would impress on the leadership in the nation to listen and be open and ready to receive godly counsel.

Miracles

> "'Do not stop him,' Jesus said. 'No one who does
> a miracle in my name can in the next moment
> say anything bad about me for whoever is not
> against us is for us'" (Mark 9:39-40).

The disciples had told Jesus they saw a man driving out
demons in Jesus's name. They told him to stop because he
was not one of the disciples. But Jesus told him, "Do not
stop him." Did you notice that Jesus called it a "miracle" to
drive out demons? It is by the name of Jesus that we have
the authority. Without Jesus, we would not have authority.

As Christians who have faith in Him, He said that we
will do even greater things than the miracles that He did.
How can that be? He gives us authority in Jesus's name to
ask God for things so that the Father's name will be glori-
fied. And He has given us His promised Holy Spirit, who
empowers us to follow Him.

"I tell you the truth, anyone who has faith in me will
do what I have been doing. He will do even greater things
than these, because I am going to the Father" (John
14:12).

When you see people do things for God, bless them.
The disciples questioned someone who was doing miracles outside of their group, but Jesus said to not stop him.

When you see people do miracles, what do you do? The first question is this—who receives the glory for it? If it is God, then pray for them and bless them.

Daily Requests

- Pray for faith in God to increase in our lives. Ask God to remind us of His faithfulness and the ways that He has revealed Himself to us.

- Ask God to increase faith in the body of Christ and that we will ask, seek, and knock for the things that we need.

- Pray for believers in the country to be assured of their faith in God and to stand up and take a chance in their communities to make a difference for God.

Lord, we ask that You increase the faith of believers in the country. Cause them to stand up and take a chance in their communities to make a difference for You.

Disentangle

> "No one engaged in warfare entangles himself with the affairs of this life, that he may please him who enlisted him as a soldier" (2 Timothy 2:4, NKJV).

Are we engaged in warfare? Of what kind? What do you struggle with most in your life? Is it pride, selfishness, or priorities? We all have struggles. Our personalities *and* our backgrounds both have an effect in what our struggles may be. But God's grace is sufficient, and He makes a way of escape for us. If you struggle with lust or greed, think of ways that you can "disentangle" yourself. What can you proactively do that will help?

What does the Word of God say? Here it says that "no one engaged in warfare entangles himself with the affairs of this life." Entangling refers to sin or compromise that is difficult to free ourselves from. We are not to become consumed with the affairs of this life. How often do we find it difficult to make the time that we need to pray? How about reading or memorizing God's Word? Store up the Word of God in your heart that you will be equipped for various trials that come your way.

Also, make the time to pray early. Cut it out early in your day and make it a habit. Take the time to pray. The rest of your day will benefit. As we give to God the first part of our day, our money, and our time, He makes the rest of it stretch further. He blesses it and is able to make all grace abound that you will have what you need at all times. Give to God the first. Place God as the first priority.

Daily Requests

- Ask God to reveal His will to you and your family or loved ones.

- Ask God to provide workers in the harvest fields and to draw others to Christ.

- Ask God to guide the course of the nation and bless His churches and the leaders of them with His will.

Lord, we ask that You stir in the hearts of Your people and provide workers in the harvest fields. Give them open doors of opportunities and draw people to Christ.

Obey in Love for God

> "You may ask me for anything in my name, and
> I will do it. If you love me, you will obey what
> I command. And I will ask the Father, and he
> will give you another Counselor to be with you
> forever—the Spirit of truth" (John 14:14-17).

Have you ever had a time when you asked God for something and His answer was an impression on your conscience for you to do it? Have you ever prayed for peace in a family and you ended up being the person who was an answer to the prayer? God works in mysterious ways.

Ask God to work. Ask Him for anything in Jesus's name, and He will do it. If it is within His will, He will do it. He hears and answers. If we love God, we also choose to obey. He gives us His counselor (the Holy Spirit) who is also the Spirit of truth. What we do not understand, we can ask God for. Ask Him for His truth.

Ask God to give you a measure of His heart for the lost—for those who have not accepted Christ. Ask Him for compassion to love them. It is the love of God that leads sinners to repentance. He must reveal His love to them, and many times it is also through His people that He reveals it. Ask God to give you a heart for the lost that will glorify His name and will be a witness for Him.

Daily Requests

- Ask God to breathe a breath of life into you, your marriage, your family, and those around you.

- Ask God to reveal to the lost His love and His goodness.

- Pray for the leadership in the nation to realize that the ways of God are best.

Lord, we ask that You work in the hearts and lives of leaders in the nation and that they will realize that Your ways are best and follow You.

Fight the Good Fight

> "Fight the good fight of the faith. Take hold of
> the eternal life to which you were called when
> you made your good confession in the presence
> of many witnesses" (1 Timothy 6:12).

Are we in a battle? Are we required to fight? What is it
that we fight? We battle our own flesh, our own fears,
and our own natural desires. We battle the ways of the
world—the commercials and advertisements that tell us
that we have to have money to succeed. We battle the
devil that constantly nags us about our lack of success.

Which desire or fear do you struggle with the most?
The Word of God tells us to conquer our fears with faith
and to fight the good fight of the faith. We are to lay hold
of the eternal life that God has called us to. We are to be
concerned with the will of God and pleasing Him more
than the money, possessions, or prestige of the world.

When we become Christians, we choose to follow
God rather than worldly ways. We choose God. We
choose Christ and determine to place the things of this
world below what Christ calls us to. Follow God. Place
Him first. Take time for Him and the things of Him, and
you will surely be blessed by God and receive the greatest

fulfillment you can have. For the things of this world are passing away, but the blessings of God last.

Daily Requests

- Seek God to give you what you need.

- Ask God to open the hearts of His people to His priorities, His ways, and His truth.

- Ask God to reveal Himself, His truth, and His love to people in the nation that they will submit fully to God.

Lord, we ask that You to draw us to You. Reveal our need for You and provide for our needs. We ask for the good gifts that You have for us.

Pray for Your Enemies

"Bless those who curse you, pray for those who mistreat you" (Luke 6:28).

What do you do when people mistreat you or speak ill about you? What is your first reaction when they cause you difficulty? Anger is a normal reaction, but the Word of God also says to pray for those who mistreat you. You are to bless those who curse you. It is normal, at times, for people to disagree with you. They may mean well but be ignorant. Remember that people also disagreed with Jesus and spoke ill about Him.

So when this happens, choose to bless them. Pray for them. Ask God to pour out His blessing upon them and reveal Himself to them. Remember that the enemy, the devil, is one who also attempts to bring accusations against people to cause difficulty. Our battle is with the flesh, the devil, and the world. Remember that people have their own slants on their understanding.

So pray for your enemies. Pray for government. Pray for those around you, including your coworkers or neighbors to see Christ in you. Ask God to reveal Himself to them and guide and direct them. Bless them, and when people around you curse you, take it before God. Pray for them and bless them.

Daily Requests

- Ask God to reveal Himself to your enemies and convict them as needed.

- Pray for righteousness to rise up in the body of Christ.

- Pray for the lost to come to salvation and an outpouring of God's Spirit upon His people to pray them to Christ.

Lord, we ask that You cause righteousness to rise up in the body of Christ and that we will shine with Your ways and Your love.

Seek to Serve

"Sitting down, Jesus called the Twelve and said,
'If anyone wants to be first, he must be the very
last, and the servant of all'" (Mark 9:35).

The disciples had been arguing on the road about who
was the greatest. They didn't tell Jesus when He asked
them, but Jesus called the disciples to Him and taught
them. He then informed them that anyone of them who
wanted to be first must be the very last and the servant of
all. He took a child in His arms and said, "Whoever welcomes one of these little children in my name welcomes
me; and whoever welcomes me does not welcome me but
the one who sent me" (Mark 9:37).

So often, we think that to be great in the kingdom of
God is to be the person who is, according to public view,
the most important or respected. But Jesus didn't view
it this way. He said if you want to be first—then serve.
Become a servant and follow Christ in it. Serve God and
serve where there is opportunity to serve. This is the way
that we reveal the love of God to others.

Where there is a need, reach out and offer to help.
Follow the leading of the Holy Spirit. Ask Him to open
your eyes to opportunities and to lead you by the power

of His precious Spirit. As we fulfill our call in the body of Christ, we find our greatest fulfillment.

Daily Requests

- Ask God to open doors of opportunity to serve Him.

- Ask God to build in His body of believers a willingness and eagerness to serve.

- Pray for the lost in the nation so that people will be available to be the arms and legs of Jesus and help them in their needs.

Lord, we ask that Your Spirit would draw the lost in the nation to You. We ask that Your people will be the arms and legs of Jesus and help them in their needs.

Do Not Be Overcome

"Do not be overcome by evil, but overcome evil with good" (Romans 12:21).

God's Word also says to hate evil and love good. We abhor evil. One could also say it this way: Do not be overcome by sin, but overcome sin with good. Overcome it with the opposite. Rather than avoiding sin, turn to the Word of God and say, "This saith the Lord, do not lust… This saith the Lord, do not be arrogant…" (Romans 11:20). And the list goes on. Overcome temptations and evil with that which is good. Put something good in the place.

Do not leave an empty area once sin is avoided or removed. You must also fill it with a love for God for His Word and for what is righteous, pure, and right. Ask God to fill your heart with a love for good and remove hidden things. If you remove a relationship that is ungodly, replace it with God and His truth.

"Love must be sincere. Hate what is evil; cling to what is good" (Romans 12:9).

Overcome evil with good. Do not leave a void where sin was but rather push sin out and keep it out by obeying the Word of God. Cling to what is good. Replace it with what is good and righteous and holy and pure. Be involved in activities that give God glory. Serve others. Love God and purify your hearts.

Daily Requests

- Ask God to give you grace to handle what you need for daily tasks.

- Ask God to reach out to the unsaved people around us to woo them to salvation and open their eyes and ears to truth and love.

- Pray for Christians in the nation to rise up boldly and speak the truth in love.

Lord, we ask for Your grace in our lives that we will be able to handle what we need for the daily tasks. Grant us an extra measure of Your grace and enablement to overcome evil with good.

Healing on the Sabbath

> "Jesus said to them, 'My Father is always at his work to this very day, and I, too, am working'" (John 5:17).

Jesus healed a man on the Sabbath. The Jews were upset about it because it was done on the Sabbath. They cared more about following a list of rules and regulations than about a man who needed healing. Jesus cared about the man who had been lame for thirty-eight years and had not made it to the healing pool.

Then the Jews were upset that the man picked up his mat and carried it on the Sabbath. Jesus was concerned about his welfare. He loved people. We are also to follow His example and love people. Jesus gave the Jews this answer, "I tell you the truth, the Son can do nothing by himself; he can do only what he sees his Father doing, because whatever the Father does the Son also does" (John 5:19).

Jesus was obedient to the Father. We are also to be obedient to God's leading in our lives. He never goes wrong. Disobedience has consequences. That is the natural law that is in place. Obedience results in blessings. God's ways are best. If you wonder if an impression you have is God's leading, look at the Word of God to see if it agrees. Also, ask the Lord to strengthen it if it is from Him and to take away the impression if it is not of Him. Seek the counsel of others, as well.

Daily Requests

- Ask God to strengthen His Word in your lives.

- Pray for the body of Christ to hear the voice of God and to follow.

- Ask God to direct the hearts of leaders in the nation.

Lord, we ask that Your people, the body of Christ, would listen to Your voice in their lives. We ask that You would enable us to follow You and be steadfast for You.

The Lord is Near

> "What other nation is so great as to have their gods near them the way the Lord our God is near us whenever we pray to him?" (Deuteronomy 4:7).

Even in the Old Testament, God was faithful to answer and be near to His people when they prayed. So also in the New Testament and today God hears and answers. There is no other god that answers the way that God, the God of the Bible, answers.

When has God answered your prayers? Ask specifically for things and date when you asked. Then you can continue to ask daily for the answers. When you receive them, write them down. Keep a journal of your requests and the answers. It will encourage you in days to come.

God answers prayer. John 14:14 says, "You may ask me for anything in my name, and I will do it." Jesus told us to ask in His name. Ask for God's will in the nation, in our communities, and our family.

Daily Requests

- Ask God to pour out His Holy Spirit upon us and revive and change us.

- Pray for the unsaved to be wooed by the Holy Spirit into a personal relationship with God.

- Ask God to pour out His Spirit upon the nation to convict people of sin.

Lord, we ask that You would woo those who do not know You by Your Holy Spirit. Draw them into love and truth so that they will come to a saving knowledge and relationship with You.

Stir Up Love and Good Works

"Let us hold fast the confession of our hope without wavering, for He who promised is faithful. And let us consider one another in order to stir up love and good works" (Hebrews 10:23-24, NKJV).

We are to have faith and hold fast the confession of our hope without wavering. God is faithful. He is faithful and true. Then because of our faith and hope we are to encourage one another in God's ways and to produce good fruit. We are to work out our salvation. We are to act on what God has spoken to our hearts. We are to have good works. We are not to sit idly by.

Jesus said in John 10:32, "Many good works I have shown you from My Father." Jesus is our example, and He helped the poor and the needy and stepped out to do good works. He healed, and He preached. He ate at the tax collector's house and reached out to the Samaritan woman. He obeyed God.

What can we do to encourage one another to stir up love and good works?

Daily Requests

- Pray for hope to come in your families, marriages, your life, and your loved ones.

- Ask God to encourage Christians to hold fast their confession and encourage one another.

- Pray for Christian leaders in the nation to be strong in the Lord and pure.

Lord, we ask that You would strengthen Your leaders in the nation. Strengthen them in the power of Your Spirit and lead them in purity and love for You.

Son-ship

> "Because those who are led by the Spirit of God are sons of God. For you did not receive a spirit that makes you a slave again to fear, but you received the Spirit of son-ship. And by him we cry, 'Abba, Father'" (Romans 8:14-16).

We are the children of God if we have accepted Christ's gift on the cross. We receive the precious Holy Spirit and are to be "led by the Spirit of God." The verse goes on to say that those who are "led by the Spirit of God" are "sons of God." The Spirit of God leads the children of God.

We did not receive a spirit that makes us afraid or overcome with fear; rather, we received a Spirit of son-ship, of adoption. By the Spirit of God, we cry out, "Daddy, Father." We have been brought into son-ship with God. He is our daddy. He is our God. He is the one who knows us through and through, and we can come to God anytime and anywhere.

As God's children—His sons and daughters—we receive the benefits of having God as our Father. His Spirit confirms with our spirit that we are His children. So we are also receiving an inheritance with Christ. We share in the sufferings that He suffered in this world so that we may also share in his glory. We have the Spirit of

God living within us and working to lead us, counsel us, guide us, and direct us in His plans and purposes, which are for our good, as well.

Daily Requests

- Ask God to reveal to you the good things that He has for you in Christ.

- Pray for a revelation of His will to come to pastors and churches.

- Ask God to change the heart of America and that He will visit us and change us to love Him first and love one another.

Lord, we ask that You open our eyes and minds to the good things that You have for us in Christ. Give us understanding.

You Are Not Alone

"He who dwells in the shelter of the Most High will rest in the shadow of the Almighty. I will say of the Lord, 'He is my refuge and my fortress, my God, in whom I trust.' Surely He will save you from the fowler's snare and from the deadly pestilence. He shall cover you with His feathers, and under His wings you shall take refuge; His truth shall be your shield and buckler" (Psalms 91:1-3).

We are to dwell in the shelter—in the protection of the Lord who is above all. Then we will rest in the shadow of the Almighty. We will stay close to Him as He watches over us. God cares for us. He covers us with His protection, and under His wings we take refuge. We stay where He has placed us.

His truth is our shield and buckler. What is His truth? His truth is that we are part of the body of Christ. We are members of the body and are not alone. God is with us and His family—the body of believers who are also called Christians are here. God covers us and protects us.

God loves us and desires good for us. How often have we heard that? It is true. He desires good. Where do you find peace? That is one way to recognize what the will of

God is. The peace of God follows the will of God. Do you have more peace in staying with His people? Then stay with them. Allow God to lead you. Allow Him to guide you and direct you. He is faithful to the end.

Daily Requests

- Ask God to reveal Himself to you through His body of believers.

- Ask God to guide and direct and shelter His people from temptations and sin.

- Pray for the future of the nation and that God will bring revival and awakening in the nation.

Lord, we ask that You guide and direct Your people. Shelter us and protect us from temptation and sin. Show us the way around them.

The Counselor

> "But I tell you the truth: It is for your good
> that I am going away. Unless I go away, the
> Counselor will not come to you; but if I go, I
> will send him to you. When he comes, he will
> convict the world of guilt in regard to sin and
> righteousness and judgment" (John 16:7-8).

Jesus was telling His disciples that He was going to be leaving. His disciples had to expect something. Jesus promised when He would leave, the Holy Spirit, the Counselor would be with them. The Holy Spirit is our counselor. He is the one who is able to give us perfect counsel.

The Holy Spirit is the one who convicts people of guilt in regard to sin and righteousness and judgment. If you ever wonder how to pray for leaders, whether political or not, ask God to counsel them in the ways to go. Ask God to convict them to do what is best, and if they are not Christians and do not follow godly ways, ask God to convict them of sin and righteousness. It is the Holy Spirit who is able to do it best.

Have you ever felt your conscience pricked about your need to reach out to the unsaved around you? It is surely the Holy Spirit who does it. He brings conviction of sin and righteousness and counsels us in the way to go. He is our counselor. Ask Him to give you direction and counsel daily.

Daily Requests

- Ask God to give you direction and counsel daily.

- Ask God to counsel pastors in the way to go and to prick their conscience when needed.

- Pray for the leaders of the nation to have their conscience pricked as needed in regard to sin and righteousness.

Lord, we ask that you would counsel pastors in the way to go. Reveal your will and your way to them. Open their eyes and, when needed, prick their conscience to change.

If You Love One Another

"A new command I give you: Love one another. As I have loved you, so you must love one another. By this all men will know that you are my disciples, if you love one another" (John 13:34-35).

If we love God, we will also love one another. It is a commitment to look out for the welfare of one another. It is a relational commitment to act in a way that is loving. When we struggle, we remember that we have God to ask for help.

By this will all men know that we follow Jesus—if we love one another. Love is greater than judgment. Love is the word that describes the reason why God sent His only Son to come to us and to reveal Himself to us and to make a way for us to live eternally with Him. Love is the beginning. Love is the key.

If you are bickering with your family or other Christians—stop. The world will look at us and be drawn to Christ by our love. If we have love for other people, we are obeying God. Spend time with others and love them. Reach out to the lost and reveal God's love to them. Shine and be different so they see Christ in us.

Daily Requests

- Ask God to give you ideas for sharing your faith with others.

- Pray for the children of God to love one another without bickering or un-forgiveness.

- Pray for people in the world to be drawn to God's love and truth and receive Him as their Savior and Lord.

Lord, we pray that You will give us creative ideas for sharing our faith with others. Show us the ways that we can be a light and example for You.

The Ways of God

"Oh, the depth of the riches of the wisdom and knowledge of God! How unsearchable his judgments, and his paths beyond tracing out! Who has known the mind of the Lord? Or who has been his counselor?" (Romans 11:33-34).

God's ways are always best. His wisdom and knowledge are beyond our understanding. His judgments are perfect. What He decides is perfect. Has God called you into something that is by faith? God, through the ages, has always called His people to a life of faith. His ways are beyond tracing out. We are to love God and follow Him by faith.

If you want to know more, read God's Word and ask Him to reveal wisdom and knowledge. Begin to ask God and continue to ask Him to give you what you desire that glory will come to His name through it.

"If any of you lacks wisdom, he should ask God, who gives generously to all without finding fault, and it will be given to him" (James 1:5).

Ask God for godly wisdom for yourself and continue to ask it for your leaders and even the leaders of your church. True wisdom is found with God. The world and all its ways are passing away. But God's ways remain and last.

Daily Requests

- Ask God to provide for your needs and give you the wisdom to do what is right.

- Ask God to shine His love and truth through the body of Christ to the unsaved.

- Pray for the Holy Spirit to convict people in the nation of their need for Him.

Lord, we ask You to shine Your life, love, and truth through Your people, Christ's body, to the unsaved.

Very Small Gift

"Jesus sat down opposite the place where the offerings were put and watched the crowd putting their money into the temple treasury. Many rich people threw in large amounts. But a poor widow came and put in two very small copper coins, worth only a fraction of a penny. Calling his disciples to him, Jesus said, "I tell you the truth, this poor widow has put more into the treasury than all the others…" (Mark 12:41-43).

Jesus sat down and watched people as they gave their tithes or offerings and commented on the least of all these. God sees the heart of the issue. How often we judge people by what we see on the outside, but really, it is the *heart* that is the issue. What do we give to God? Is it our heart or just money? Hopefully we do both. Give to God our tithes and offerings out of our love for God.

How many people gave large amounts of money. They gave out of their wealth, but a poor woman gave her two copper coins, and Jesus commented on her the most. She gave all she could give. She gave all she had to live on as it says in the next verse.

Do not compare yourself with others. We are not to measure ourselves by others but rather by the Word of God. Give to God your tithes because of your love for God.

Daily Requests

- Pray for wisdom and revelation to know His ways.

- Ask God to give His children a generosity in heart and to give to Him.

- Pray for leaders in the nation to love righteousness and shun evil.

Lord, we ask You to work in the hearts and lives of leaders in the nation. Place in them a love for righteousness and the desire and courage to avoid evil.

Cast Your Bread

> "Cast your bread upon the waters, for after many days you will find it again" (Ecclesiastes 11:1).

Take your chances. Throw your bread out there, for you do not know which dream will work out. Risks are a part of life.

The Word says that if you cast your bread upon the waters, you will find it again. Do you feel that God is leading you to step out of your comfort zone? Step out, and you will grow more comfortable as you continue. Take a risk and obey God. One small step in tiny increments is more than no step at all.

Make your goals. Cast your bread upon the waters and see where it goes. We don't always know if something will work out or if success will come, but if we never try, we are assured of one result—nothing. A few verses down in the passage, it says, "Whoever watches the wind will not plant; whoever looks at the clouds will not reap" (Ecclesiastes 11:4).

Trust the Lord and try. Have faith. Share your faith with someone. Cast your bread upon the waters and allow God to use it.

KARI BITZ

Daily Requests

- Ask God for success and favor in your endeavors.

- Pray for the body of Christ to step out in faith and follow God.

- Ask God to pour His love and truth into the lives of people in the nation and to turn them to Him.

Lord, we ask You for success and favor in all we do. Increase our faith to step out and obey.

Make a Difference

"You are the salt of the earth. But if the salt loses its saltiness, how can it be made salty again? It is no longer good for anything, except to be thrown out and trampled by men" (Matthew 5:13).

How do we become salty or flavorful? It is by the Spirit of the living God. He is and was and is to come. He is the one who gives life the abundance and joy that we desire. As we come into His will, we experience the abundant life and joy and richness and prosperity of soul that we desire.

It is by the Spirit of the living God that we are made different. We must be led by His Spirit. Draw near to God, and He will draw near to you. Accept Him as your Lord and Savior. Allow Him to lead you and guide you and direct you and you will be led into a life of saltiness and love for God and the lost. Read the Word of God. Allow Him to speak through His Word. His Word brings truth.

Allow God to make you salty and different.

Daily Requests

- Allow God to lead you into His will today.

- Pray for the lost to see the saltiness in our lives and realize the difference Christ makes.

- Pray for the leaders in the nation to be drawn to God through Christ by the Holy Spirit and though the example of Christians.

Lord, we pray that non-Christians around us would see the saltiness in our lives. We pray that they realize their need for Christ and desire Your Spirit and presence in their lives.

Rejoice and be Glad!

> "Blessed are you when people insult you, perse-
> cute you and falsely say all kinds of evil against
> you because of me. Rejoice and be glad, because
> great is your reward in heaven, for in the same
> way they persecuted the prophets who were
> before you" (Matthew 5:11-12).

Do you fear people saying the wrong thing about you or
persecuting you because of your faith in Christ? Do you
realize that you will be reward for it? Of course we are to
be Christ-like and not go out of our way to offend people,
and yet we are to speak the truth in love. Jesus spoke truth
in love. The Word of God is powerful and effective. We
can take the Word of God and apply it to situations for
people whether or not we actually tell them initially that
it is the Word of God that we are sharing. Be led by the
Spirit of God and do not fear sharing your faith or the
Word of God.

But if and when you are persecuted, which as a follower of Christ you will be at times unless you hide your
faith from everyone, remember that you have a reward in
heaven coming. Rejoice and be glad that people notice a
difference. Be an example of Jesus as His follower and let
it be a godly example that people see.

Rejoice and pray for them to be convicted of sin and come to an understanding of God's love for them. Ask God to reveal truth in love to them. Love them in spite of insults or scorns. Be glad that people notice a difference. Let it be a loving and godly difference.

Daily Requests

- Ask God to reveal Himself to you and speak to you today.

- Ask God to reveal truth in love through His people's lives.

- Pray for national repentance and that great awakening will come in the nation through the living Spirit of God.

Lord, we ask that You bring national repentance. We ask that You pour out Your Spirit and life upon us and awaken people to their need for You.

Saving Power of God

"Now I know that the Lord saves his anointed; he answers him from his holy heaven with the saving power of his right hand" (Psalms 20:6).

Do you know God saves his anointed? How many trials had David been through when he wrote this? He was known for praying to God for help. "He answers him from his holy heaven." God answers when we pray. He hears and answers. He cares.

Have you ever had a time when you cried out to God for a period of time? Did God answer? Remember the ways that God has answered in the past and the ways that you have responded. Our God is a faithful God.

Will you obey God no matter what? The Lord saves. He delivers. He makes a way. Look through the stories of the Bible and see God answer His people when they pray.

"Some trust in chariots, and some in horses; but we will remember the name of the Lord our God" (Psalms 20:7).

Daily Requests

- Ask God to encourage our hearts in His ways and open our eyes to salvation.

- Pray for the lost to come to salvation and place their faith in God.

- Ask God to bring revival and spiritual awakening in the nation for His glory.

Lord, we ask that You encourage our hearts in Your ways. Open our eyes to Your salvation and our hearts to trust You.

The Compassion of God upon Us

"As a father has compassion on his children, so the Lord has compassion on those who fear him" (Psalms 103:13).

What does it mean to fear God? Is it to shake in our boots when we come to Him? To fear God is to have a healthy respect of Him. We love Him and respect Him, His ways, and His desires for our lives. He is a loving Father who has perfect sight into our lives.

We see in part. God sees the whole. He has compassion on us. What are your needs? Talk to Him as a loving Father. Come before Him and lift up your needs before Him. Jesus prayed, in the Lord's Prayer, "Give us today our daily bread" (Matthew 6:11). He knows that we have needs. He desires to fill those needs. Ask Him for them. He is a compassionate Father.

"For he knows how we are formed, he remembers that we are dust" (Psalms 103:14).

God knows how we are formed. He remembers that we were formed from dust and return to dust when we die. It is God who is with us. He is the one who knows our weaknesses and has great compassion on us. Follow Him where He calls. Tell Him your needs.

Daily Requests

- Ask for your daily bread. Ask Him to meet your specific needs.

- Pray for God's people to turn to God in prayer and fasting.

- Ask God to turn the nation around by His mercy and His power.

Lord, we ask that You would encourage and stimulate people in the nation to unite in prayer and fasting. Give your children a passion to pray and fast.

Sacrifice with Thanksgiving

"But I, with a song of thanksgiving, will sacrifice to you. What I have vowed I will make
good. Salvation comes from the LORD" (Jonah
2:9).

Jonah had disregarded God's voice to go to Ninevah. He
boarded a boat going in the opposite direction. The storm
that arose threatened to take the lives of all on the boat,
so Jonah told them that he was running from God. They
asked what they should do, and he replied to throw him
overboard. When they did, God sent a big fish to swallow
him and put him on a road to repentance of heart.

A road was paved in the belly of the fish that turned
Jonah from running away from God to obeying Him. We
do not always know the distance that we are running from
God. When Jonah committed to obey God, the Lord
commanded the fish to spit Jonah out onto the dry land.

Jonah then went with God's Word to the city that God
desired and was obedient. The people obeyed, and a city
was saved from God's judgment and destruction. What
have we obeyed God on? Ask God if there is something
that God desires you to do that you haven't yet.

Daily Requests

- Pray that we will be faithful to obey and love God and walk in faith.

- Ask God to encourage His people to obey.

- Pray for children in the nation to have workers in their lives to bring them to Christ.

Lord, we pray for children in the nation to have workers provided in their lives to bring them to Christ. We ask that You send out people to work with children.

Knows Our Names

> "One of the two who heard John speak, and followed Him, was Andrew, Simon Peter's brother. He first found his own brother Simon, and said to him, 'We have found the Messiah' (which is translated, the Christ). And he brought him to Jesus. Now when Jesus looked at him, He said, 'You are Simon the son of Jonah. You shall be called Cephas' (which is translated, a Stone)" (John 1:40-42, NKJV).

Andrew heard John speak and followed Jesus. We are to be people who lead others to Christ. When they are around us, we are to be people who point them to Christ. Andrew told Simon Peter that he had found the Messiah. What does *messiah* mean? It refers to a deliverer. He will deliver us from our sins, for one. Jesus is the Messiah, the one who the Jews were waiting for.

Andrew brought his brother to Jesus. When Jesus saw him, He knew all about him. He knew his future and who he would be in the church. He knew his past, and gave him a name that was descriptive of his activity for the kingdom of God. He was to be a rock that the church would be built on, and the gates of hell would not overcome it (Matthew 16:18).

Do you know that God knows your name? He knows your beginnings and your future. Your past is in His hands to work through to bring forth gold. Your future is also in His hands, as well as your present, to bring forth good and not evil. He is your messiah if you accept Him. He is your deliverer.

Daily Requests

- Ask God to reveal Himself to you, mighty to save.

- Ask God to deliver us from every evil work and bring us safely into His heavenly kingdom (2 Timothy 4:18).

- Pray for unsaved leaders in the nation to accept Christ as their Lord and Savior.

Lord, we ask that You reveal Yourself to us. Give us an understanding of You as our Messiah and Deliverer.

Knowledge and Understanding

"To these four young men God gave knowledge and understanding of all kinds of literature and learning. And Daniel could understand visions and dreams of all kinds" (Daniel 1:17).

Have dreams come to an end? Not at all. Do we ask God for them? He is able to give them. God gave visions to people in the New Testament as well. He is able to speak through them. Sometimes they are visions in our mind's eye that take hold of a passion and give us direction. He is able to lead us and direct us.

Do you notice what the Word of God says? God gave knowledge and understanding. The four men had been taken into captivity when Jerusalem was overcome by their enemy. They were trained for three years in the ways of the Babylonians, but they had determined not to leave their one true God. They did not defile themselves. And God blessed them. Even in a foreign land where fine drink and food and probably possessions were offered to them, they remained faithful to God and stood fast.

Do you need wisdom? Do you need understanding? God gives to those who ask. Stand fast in your faith and choose to follow Him. Then ask for these things as you need. It is the one and true God who gives wisdom and understanding beyond man's means. The passage here continues and says, "In every matter of wisdom and understanding about which the king questioned them, he found them ten times better than all the magicians and enchanters in his whole kingdom" (verse 20). True wisdom and understanding comes from God. Follow Him and ask Him for it.

Daily Requests

- Ask God to encourage your heart in His ways of peace.

- Pray for wisdom and understanding that only God can give to be evident in our families and communities.

- Ask God to grant supernatural wisdom to the leaders in the nation.

Lord, we ask that You give us wisdom and understanding. Tell us unsearchable things we do not know.

Brought Back to Life

"But Peter put them all out, and knelt down and prayed. And turning to the body he said, 'Tabitha, arise.' And she opened her eyes, and when she saw Peter she sat up" (Acts 9:40, NKJV).

Do you think miracles bring people to Christ?

Tabitha was a woman who was described as "full of good works and charitable deeds" (Acts 9:36, NKJV). The people loved her. When she became sick and died, they washed her and laid her in an upper room. When they heard that Peter was near, they sent two men to him to ask him to come quickly. And Peter went.

When he came to Tabitha, he sent everyone out of the room, knelt down before God, and prayed. Then he turned to her body and said, "Tabitha, arise." Had He asked God for mercy? Had He asked God to intervene for other's sake? We don't know for sure. What we do know is that God answered and delivered Tabitha from death.

As word spread, many believed in the Lord. It resulted in people coming to Christ. Ask God for miracles. He is able.

Daily Requests

- Ask God to reveal His hand of mercy in our lives and work miracles in and through us.

- Ask God to send out workers into the harvest field and to bring the Word to them.

- Pray for an abundance of rain (a spiritual refreshing) in the nation.

Lord, we ask that You reveal Your hand of mercy in our lives. We ask You to work miracles in and through our lives.

The Unfailing Love of the Lord

> "O Israel, put your hope in the Lord, for with the Lord is unfailing love and with Him is full redemption" (Psalms 130:7).

God is a loving God. He is a merciful God. He is a holy and just God. He loves to deliver us from sin. He has not only cancelled the debt against us but God also delivered us from the control of darkness. He has set us free to live for Him. In Him are joy, life, and peace.

What is abundant redemption? It is a cancelling of the debt that was against us from our sin. God paid the price fully. He reached out and did what we could not do for ourselves. How often have people thought of God as a judgmental, harsh God? He is not unloving; rather, He is full of love. He is the God who saves, the God who hears, and the God who reaches us when we cannot fix ourselves.

Put your hope in the Lord, for He is rich in mercy. Can you think of times when God has worked His mercy in your life? List them. Think on them and thank God for His mercy.

Daily Requests

- Ask God to pour out His love and mercy upon your life and others that need it.

- Pray for people to come closer to Christ and to love Him with all their hearts and minds.

- Ask for open doors to teach, preach, and share Christ in the nation.

Lord, we ask that You reveal Yourself as our daddy who loves us and is perfect in understanding. Draw people to You, Lord, and to love You with all their hearts and mind.

Store Your Provisions

> "Go to the ant, you sluggard; consider its ways and be wise! It has no commander, no overseer or ruler, yet it stores its provisions in summer and gathers its food at harvest" (Proverbs 6:6-8).

Look at the ant. Although it has no commander or overseer, it prepares for the seasons. The ant knows what season is coming. It motivates itself to work and be prepared. We are to be hard workers for the Lord. We are also to set an example in our communities and around the work environment. We are to be people of faith.

Do we know the seasons and the times? We are to plan and work accordingly. Work hard and gather or plant for the summer months because you will be blessed beyond measure if you work hard.

All we can do is our best. Consider the ant who stores and gathers in season. It prepares and plans accordingly. Be self motivated. Set your goals and follow through. Do your best to finish what you have started. Set an example in speech and in conduct in your neighborhood. Be where God has planted you and thrive.

Daily Requests

- Ask God to encourage our hearts.

- Ask God to give vision and direction to His people.

- Pray for the nation so that the Holy Spirit will be poured out upon us and bring revival.

Lord, we ask that You pour out Your Spirit upon us and bring revival in the nation. Revive us, Lord and impassion us for You.

Bless and Do Not Curse

> "Bless those who persecute you; bless and do not curse. Rejoice with those who rejoice; mourn with those who mourn" (Romans 12:14-15).

How often do we bless those who persecute us? It is the example that God gives us to follow. We are to bless them and offer a soft answer. Truth in love is the call of God. The love softens our answer. Truth does not compromise.

Bless and do not curse. Bless others. Ask God to bless others. Act in ways that will bless others. Romans 12:20 says, "If your enemy is hungry, feed him; if he is thirsty, give him something to drink. In doing this, you will heap burning coals on his head."

We are to not be overcome by evil but overcome evil with good. This is the example that we are to have before others and God. He watches the way of the righteous. Ask God for ideas and ways to bless others when they are difficult to bless.

Daily Requests

- Pray for more of God's grace in your life.

- Pray for the unsaved to be won over by our good deeds and actions.

- Pray for leaders in the nation to love God and follow God.

Lord, we ask that You pour Your grace into our lives. Reveal Your grace to us and change us.

As Daniel Was Protected

> "For he is the living God and he endures for-
> ever; his kingdom will not be destroyed, his
> dominion will never end" (Daniel 6:27).

God rescues and saves; He performs signs and wonders in
the heavens and on the earth. He has rescued Daniel from
the power of the lions.

The king praised "the God of Daniel," who is able
(Daniel 6:26-27). Daniel had disobeyed the king's order
to worship no one but the king for a month. Daniel continued to worship God in front of his window three times
a day. His enemies told the king who liked Daniel but
knew that since he had issued a royal edict or decree, he
could not change it even if it meant that Daniel would be
thrown into the lions' den. So Daniel was thrown into the
lions' den for praying to his God.

What did God do? He stepped in and worked a miracle by sending an angel to protect Him from the lions.
The result was two fold. Daniel was protected from the
lions, and the king was changed. The king then praised
Daniel's God about whom he then also issued a decree
that all the people must worship Him.

God is able to work miracles in the midst of difficulties.

Daily Requests

- Pray for God to bless you with love and rejoice in His ways all of your days.

- Pray for the lost to come to salvation and be drawn to Him with quick resolve to obey quickly!

- Pray for the righteous to rise up in the nation and be an example for Him.

Lord, we ask You to work miracles in and through Your body. Stir up the gifts that You have given and work miracles by Your Spirit.

Follow Jesus

> "As Jesus walked beside the Sea of Galilee, he saw Simon and his brother Andrew casting a net into the lake, for they were fishermen. "Come, follow me," Jesus said, "and I will make you fishers of men." At once they left their nets and followed him" (Mark 1:16-18).

Jesus called Simon and Andrew to follow Him. And they left their nets behind. We are to do the same. Where God calls, we are to follow. We are to be fishers of men. What does that mean? We are to draw others to Christ. That is our call.

Jesus called these two men from the life they were used to, to serve God and draw others to Him. They became servants, and "at once" they left their nets and followed Jesus. Is there some way that God is calling you into ministry? Is He calling you to change your neighborhood? Is there a way that you can reach out to the children in your area and share Christ with them? Some people start Bible studies and invite their unsaved friends to come. Listen to the Holy Spirit's leading and participate in what He is calling you to do.

Daily Requests

- Ask God to give you a heart for others in your area that need Christ.

- Pray for truth to become evident and that we will obey God's leading and direction.

- Pray for the soul of the nation to heal and be changed by God's mercy.

Lord, we ask You to heal the soul of the nation and to tenderize the affections of its people to You. We ask for Your mercy to change us.

Pray Always

> "…praying always with all prayer and supplication in the Spirit, being watchful to this end with all perseverance and supplication for all the saints" (Ephesians 6:18, NKJV).

What are we to do? Pray always is the first directive. We are to pray always. What do we pray? Pray for God's will to come. What is God's will? Ask God to bless and protect you and your family. Ask God to reveal His love to you and your loved ones and coworkers. Ask God to pour out His Spirit upon you and those near you to bring people to Christ and to accomplish His will.

Also, we are to be watchful or alert with all perseverance and intercession or supplication for all the saints. Pray for one another. Be watchful for one another. Love one another. Encourage each other in prayer. Pray for the larger body of Christ (all the saints) and that God will fulfill His purposes in the body. Continue to pray and ask of God.

Daily Requests

- Ask God to provide for your needs and give you a passion for prayer.

- Ask God to stir up the gifts in the body of Christ—the church.

- Pray for encouragement to come over Christian leaders in the nation that they will have courage and boldness to speak with power.

Lord, we ask You to provide for our needs and give us a passion for prayer. Strengthen us and lead us in prayer for Your glory.

Not Live on Bread Alone

> "Jesus answered, 'It is written: "Man does not live on bread alone, but on every word that comes from the mouth of God"'" (Matthew 4:4).

Do we survive off of food? Or do we live with the Word of God? Which is more important? Did you know that in fasting, as Jesus was doing in this instance, the devil came to Him directly and challenged His decision to fast? If He was tempted in this way, so we can expect to be tempted when we fast, as well. Remember that food is not what truly satisfies. It may be easy to grab but does not have long term sustenance.

When you are tempted to overeat, do what Jesus did in this case and repeat the verse out loud, "It is written, 'Man shall not live by bread alone, but by every word that proceeds from the mouth of God.'"

That is the test. What do we do when we are in need of food? Do we run to meet it in godly ways or in ungodly ways? Ask God to show you what you do. Ask God to guide you in it. Write this verse on an index card and memorize it for the times that you may need it.

Daily Requests

- Ask God to guide you in godly ways always.

Kari Bitz

- Pray for peace in the kingdom of God so that we will live in peace with one another as God desires.

- Ask God to shake the foundations that need to be shaken and build what needs to be built in the nation.

Lord, we ask for peace in the body of Christ. Guide us into peace and love in our relationships as You desire.

Counsel of the Ungodly

> "Blessed is the man who does not walk in the counsel of the wicked or stand in the way of sinners or sit in the seat of mockers" (Psalms 1:1).

Happy and prosperous is the person that does not walk in the counsel of the ungodly. God's favor rests upon you when you do not follow after ungodly ways or stand in the way of sinners. We do not follow their ways or become comfortable with their sin; rather, we follow after God instead. Do not become entangled with those who scorn on God's laws.

"But his delight is in the law of the Lord, and on his law he meditates day and night" (Psalms 1:1).

What does this mean? We are to delight ourselves in God's Word. We are to delight in dwelling on His Word. We love God and we choose to obey His Word because God brings the blessings. He watches over the way of the righteous (verse six). He makes us stand firm and be fruitful. His laws are perfect, and the way of the Lord is right.

Trust in the Lord. Delight yourself in His Word and follow Him. Do what is right and trust the Lord, for He will make your plans prosper. Read His Word daily and think on it throughout the day. Allow your best friends to be those who love God and love His ways.

Daily Requests

- Ask God to give you a love for His Word and to bring it to mind throughout the day.

- Ask God to give understanding and revelation of His word to Christians in your community.

- Pray for the Word of the Lord to go forth and be powerful in the country.

Lord, we ask that Your Word would go forth in the nation. We ask that Your Spirit would empower it and cause it to be effective and powerful in the nation to bring godly change where needed.

Provision in Time

> "If you follow my decrees and are careful to obey my commands, I will send you rain in its season, and the ground will yield its crops and the trees of the field their fruit" (Leviticus 26:3-4).

What are the commands God gives? The first and foremost is to love God with all your heart, with all your mind, and with all your soul (Matthew 22:37). The second is to love your neighbor as yourself (Matthew 22:39). We love God first. We obey His commands. We follow Him. We give to Him in tithes and offerings. We worship God and follow after Him, and He sends His blessings. God's grace is greater than all of our sin.

Will we ever be perfect? No one is without sin, but quick repentance leads to God's presence. Obedience always brings blessings. Here, the promise is, "I will send you rain in its season, and the ground will yield its crops." There will be provision. Is there anything that God has called you to do that is coming to mind now that you haven't been faithfully doing?

Be fruitful where you are placed. Spend time with God and ask Him how to love Him where you are.

Daily Requests

- Ask God to lead you by His Spirit (Romans 8:14).

- Pray for understanding in Christians and that God will bless obedience.

- Ask God to encourage His people to share their faith in the nation.

Lord, we ask that You lead us by Your Spirit and that we will be careful to obey You, follow You, and receive the blessings that You have for us.

Be Strong and Courageous!

"Be strong and courageous, because you will lead these people to inherit the land I swore to their forefathers to give them" (Joshua 1:6).

Joshua was required to be strong and courageous. God commanded him to do so. He was required to lead the people into the Promised Land. It required strength and courage for the assignment. Do you have something in your life that requires strength and courage? God also told him, "Have I not commanded you? Be strong and courageous. Do not be terrified; do not be discouraged, for the Lord your God will be with you wherever you go" (Joshua 1:9).

While leading the Israelites, even when things looked bad, Joshua was to obey God. He was to seek God and meditate on His Word day and night and to obey it (verse eight). Then He would be prosperous and successful. The principles in God's Word are principles that bring success and prosperity of spirit. We are to be strong and courageous to do what God calls us to do.

Courageous—what is that? It is bravery that defies or challenges something. It is the state of mind or spirit that enables us to face difficulties and challenges. It acts opposite of fear. When the people turned and ran away from the challenge to drive out their enemies, Joshua was to lead them into it and face it with courage and strength. He was to wield the Word of God against the threat or difficulty. So what is the word of God? For one, it is what God has spoken in the past concerning our difficulty. What is the word that He has spoken to your heart? What does the Bible say concerning it?

Daily Requests

- Ask God to give you courage and increase your faith in Him.

- Ask God to bring thankfulness into the heart of His people and to remember His faithfulness.

- Ask God to instill courage and bravery into His leaders in the nation to do His will.

Lord, we ask You to remind us of Your faithful love. Draw us near to you and instill courage in us to obey.

Prevailing Prayer

"So Ahab went off to eat and drink, but Elijah climbed to the top of Carmel, bent down to the ground and put his face between his knees. 'Go and look toward the sea,' he told his servant. And he went up and looked. 'There is nothing there,' he said. Seven times Elijah said, 'Go back.' The seventh time the servant reported, 'A cloud as small as a man's hand is rising from the sea'" (1 Kings 18:42-44).

King Ahab went off to eat and drink, but God's prophet, Elijah, climbed to the top of a mountain and prayed to God. He not only prayed once, but he continued to pray. And he asked his servant to go and look for the cloud—a sign that his prayer was being answered. The servant went back seven times to look for the sign that his prayer was being answered. Finally, he saw the cloud that was as small as a man's hand that was rising from the sea.

Have you continued in prayer until you see the cloud or the sign of your prayer being answered? Is there a prayer that you have not continued to pray for? Elijah prayed not only once for rain; he prevailed until the answer was on the way. Do you need rain? Do you need success? Do you need enablement in an area? Begin to ask God to provide, and when he sends provision your way in the form of a person or persons or by His grace, begin to use the provision He sends.

In this case, God answered Elijah with heavy rain. Do not quit asking God to send national repentance. Your prayers are being answered daily. Look for the answer.

Daily Requests

- Ask God to lead you in ways of righteousness for His name's sake.

- Ask God to speak truth to the body of Christ and that we would be receptive to it.

- Pray for God's hand to work in the nation and to draw people to Him.

Lord, we ask You to lead us in ways of righteousness for Your name's sake. Guide us in Your ways and encourage our hearts in You.

Jesus Is the Light

> "The people living in darkness have seen a great
> light; on those living in the land of the shadow
> of death a light has dawned" (Matthew 4:16).

A great light dawned in the land. Can you imagine living
in those times? To hear the stories about Jesus and live
in the same area as He lived would have been something
to remember.

How many people in the world follow Muslim,
Buddhism, and other religions and are held in bondage
and in a certain fear and a "shadow of death"? They are
held in captivity to ways that are not God's ways. His
ways are perfect and in Christ is freedom and liberty.
"For where the Spirit of the Lord is there is freedom" (2
Corinthians 3:17).

When you look through history, the nations that follow God's principles tend to have greater blessings and
peace. Jesus was sent to proclaim freedom for the prison-
ers and to release the oppressed. Follow God, and you will
be led into liberty.

Daily Requests

- Ask God for truth to be revealed in our lives and
  His love in our relationships.

- Pray for the lost to come to salvation and be freed from the lies of the enemy.

- Ask God to bring a great light of truth in the nation that people will be drawn to Christ and His love.

Lord, we ask you to bring the lost to salvation. Open their eyes to the salvation You have for them and free them from the lies of the enemy.

Trust in the Light

> "Put your trust in the light while you have it, so that you may become sons of light" (John 12:36).

Jesus was speaking to His disciples and said this right after telling them that that He would be lifted up. He told them to put their trust in the light while they still have the light. Who is the light? Jesus is the light. He is the light of the world, and by Him we walk in the light. Trust in the light of God's Word, the revelation of His Spirit, and the counsel of His Spirit.

We are to be sons of light. We are sons and daughters of God if we have received Christ. He is the light and shines the light in the midst of the darkness to reveal truth and dispel lies. It is the light that reveals what is hidden. That which is not of God tends to hide itself. Do you remember Adam and Eve in Genesis? When they sinned is when they began to cover themselves. We are to be open and honest with God. We are to be sons of the light and not to avoid the light but are to allow God to work in our lives and shed light or truth onto the areas that need His touch.

Be open to God's truth and correction. Allow His light to shine in your life, reveal hidden areas, clean out those closets, and bring truth.

Daily Requests

- Ask God to open closet doors in our lives and reveal truth to us as needed.

- Pray for open doors of opportunity to share God with others.

- Pray for the nation and that godly leadership will rise up.

Lord, we ask that You would open doors of opportunity to share You with others. Help us to see the open doors and be faithful to share Christ.

Alpha and Omega

> "'I am the Alpha and the Omega,' says the Lord
> God, 'who is, and who was, and who is to come,
> the Almighty'" (Revelation 1:8).

Who is our God? Who is the One that we trust in, who delivers us, and who plans ahead for our lives? It is He who made us, formed us, and created us in His likeness. He is our God, and we are His kids.

It is the Lord Almighty, the Alpha and the Omega, the beginning and the end, who is and was and who is to come. Wherever we are afraid to go, He has already been. Do not fear but trust Him and He shall make this come to pass.

What the Lord has spoken to you—obey. What He has promised to do—trust and believe Him for it. Our Lord is a good God. He is a righteous God, and He cares for us. He is also the almighty, the invincible, who sees all and knows what to do to bring success. Trust in Him. Invite Him to be a part of your day and love Him, for He is your heavenly Father and your Savior.

Trust in the Lord. Whatever you do—trust.

Daily Requests

- Ask God to be with You in a real way and comfort and guide you.

- Pray for revelation on things to come in our communities and families.

- Ask God to take the body of Christ to a new level of repentance and fasting in the nation.

Lord, we ask You to give us revelation and understanding of things to come.

If God is God

> "Elijah went before the people and said, 'How long will you waver between two opinions? If the Lord is God, follow him; but if Baal is God, follow him.' But the people said nothing. Then Elijah said to them, 'I am the only one of the Lord's prophets left, but Baal has four hundred and fifty prophets...'" (1 Kings 18:21-22).

Elijah went before the people and declared that whoever's god answers their cry with fire is God. The prophets of Baal prepared a bull on an altar for their false god. They called from morning until noon with no answer or response. When Elijah mocked them that their god was deep in thought, busy, traveling, or even sleeping and needed to be awakened, the prophets of Baal shouter louder and cut their skin until they bled. There was no response even by evening.

What a scene that would have to have been. They could not impress their so-called god enough to get a response. Then Elijah said to all the people, "Come here..." He repaired the altar of the Lord, which was in ruins. He dug a trench around it, arranged the wood, cut the bull to pieces, and laid it on the wood. Then he had four large jars of water poured over the altar three times, and the water filled the trench.

Elijah stepped forward and prayed. He asked God to reveal that he was God's servant and did what God commanded. He asked God to answer so that the people knew that the Lord was God—and God answered. The fire of the Lord fell and burned up the sacrifice, the wood, the stones, and the soil and even licked up the water in the trench. The people knew that the Lord was God.

Daily Requests

- Pray that God will deliver us from the hands of the enemy.

- Ask God to reveal Himself to people in ways that reveal His sovereignty and faithfulness.

- Ask God to bring great revival in the nation that people will know that God is God.

Lord, we ask You to bring revival in the nation. Revive the hearts of people to love You more and bring repentance where needed so that we will know that You are God.

Joseph was Born

"After Rachel gave birth to Joseph, Jacob said to Laban, 'Send me on my way so I can go back to my own homeland. Give me my wives and children, for whom I have served you, and I will be on my way. You know how much work I've done for you'" (Genesis 30:25-26).

Rachel prayed for a child because she had none. So the Lord opened her womb and gave her a son. After Rachel gave birth to their son, Joseph, Jacob then requested to be on his way from his father-in-law for whom he had worked for fourteen years. Laban, the father-in-law, was not willing for him to leave but made a deal with Jacob (Joseph's father), saying that he would receive the less favorable sheep. And Jacob grew exceedingly prosperous through it.

Laban was blessed when Jacob was with him and became wealthy during the fourteen years. How many of us would stay in business with our in-laws for fourteen years? Jacob had God's blessing on him. He was the father of Joseph, whom God used mightily in the years to come. Jacob worked hard serving others, and God used the time to bless him.

Wherever you are, work heartily as for the Lord and not as unto men (Colossians 3:23). It is the Lord that will reward you, and the principles He set in place bring rewards for our hard work. As for the hard working ant or the sluggard, principles apply. Work hard and you will have ample supply. So also the sluggard will have the opposite. When God calls you out to go to another place, you will be ready with the skills and provisions that are needed.

Daily Requests

- Ask God to give you a joyful heart and right attitude so you can work for the-Lord.

- Ask God to encourage the body of Christ to shine for Him so people will see a difference in us.

- Ask God to work in the hearts and minds of people in the nation and to bring a turning to God that times of refreshing may come.

Lord, we ask that you give us joyful hearts and right attitudes as we work. Help us to work heartily as for You, Lord.

Righteous by Faith

> "I am not ashamed of the gospel, because it is the power of God for the salvation of everyone who believes: first for the Jew, then for the Gentile. For in the gospel a righteousness from God is revealed, a righteousness that is by faith from first to last, just as it is written: 'The righteous will live by faith'" (Romans 1:16-17).

Does our righteousness come from good works, or does it come through faith in Christ? We are made righteous through faith in Christ. He has become our righteousness, holiness, and redemption. We accept His gift, and we are made righteous because of our faith in Christ. The call of God upon the Christian is to believe in Christ's full payment for our sins and then to walk in His righteousness by faith. We live by faith.

How often in the Christian life do we need faith? How often we do not see very far ahead of us? He gives us enough light for the next step. Then we must rest and trust as we walk. Faith is the substance that enables us to continue. "The righteous will live by faith." Abraham was called to walk by faith, so we are also called to believe God and follow Him.

We are made right with God by faith. Are we perfect? No. We will never be. But we contend for the prize by continuing. It is faith first. Faith that is alive has actions with it. So we are made righteous by faith in Christ. That means obedience. We rise up and live by faith.

Daily Requests

- Ask God to draw us to Himself and encourage our hearts in faith.

- Ask God to increase faith in the body of Christ so that we will be faithful to His calling in our lives.

- Ask God to work repentance into the leaders of the nation that they will be turned to God for His glory.

Lord, increase our faith in You, in Your word, and in Your calling in our lives. We ask that You guide us to live by faith according to Your word. Teach us to do so.

Hope in God

> "Send forth Your light and your truth, let them guide me; let them bring me to your holy mountain and to the place where You dwell… Why are you downcast, O my soul? Why so disturbed within me? Put your hope in God, for I will yet praise Him, my Savior and my God" (Psalms 43:3, 5).

The psalmist asks God to send forth His light and His truth. They guide us. When darkness surrounds us, it is the light of God and the truth of God that blazes or points the way to go. It is the light of God's Word, God's grace, and God's presence that lights the path ahead. Have you ever felt like you were in a valley or a low place? Prepare for it before it happens. God's presence will go with You.

It is the light and truth of God that guide us along with the Holy Spirit. The love of God is upon us. Where do the light and truth of God lead us? They lead us and guide us to His presence and to the mountain of God—the holy place where He dwells.

The psalmist goes on to write a phrase that is used three times in two chapters. "Why are you downcast, O my soul?" He goes on to encourage himself to place His hope in God. He commits to look to God and to put His eyes on the goal. He continues to praise God. How often are our attitudes changed as we look to God and praise Him along the way? Take time to praise God today.

Daily Requests

- Take time to praise God.

- Ask God to encourage your heart in His love and faithfulness and that of your loved ones or family.

- Pray for the nation that God will mercifully turn people back to His ways and love Him.

Lord, we ask that your light and your truth guide us. Encourage our hearts and fill us with hope, for we are Yours.

God Loves to Pardon

> "For He has rescued us from the dominion of darkness and brought us into the kingdom of the Son He loves, in whom we have redemption, the forgiveness of sins" (Colossians 1:13-14).

God loves to pardon. He loves to forgive as we turn to Him. He loves to pull us up out of the muck and mire that sin and our own natural ways cause. He loves to protect us and shield us. As we follow His ways, we are safer than when we try to protect ourselves.

When we fail, God is at work to bring us back. He was at work even before we knew Christ. His grace was at work, and His plans were already in the making. Because of His Son, we have been rescued from the power and control of darkness. We have God's help to deliver us from every evil temptation, and we have the body of Christ to grow with.

With God and His provision, we are able to overcome temptations we could never overcome on our own. We can overcome addictions. We can overcome habits and struggles that on our own we have been powerless to do. Come before God in prayer and seek His help. Lean on Him.

Daily Requests

- Ask God to give you the enablement to do His will.

- Pray for the lost to come to know Christ and be rescued from slavery to sin.

- Pray for the leaders in the nation to be drawn to a loving God who has prepared and planned a good purpose in their lives.

Lord God, enable us to overcome the obstacles that hold us back from following You.

Do Good

"Trust in the Lord and do good; dwell in the land and enjoy safe pasture" (Psalms 37:3).

Who doesn't want to be safe and prosper? This verse tells us first to trust in the Lord, and *then* we are to do good. We are to have actions that follow and go hand-in-hand with our trust in God. If we trust the Lord, we will obey Him. We will seek His counsel and His wisdom. We will act upon what He makes known to us. We will act upon what we place our faith in. Where do we place our faith—in ourselves or in God?

Next we are to dwell in the land we are physically in and feed on His faithfulness. We live as a resident in the land where God has placed us. We settle down in it and feed on His faithfulness in His truth. If we love God, we will make it known to others by our actions. Faith without actions is dead.

The next verse continues this way: "Delight yourself in the Lord, and He will give you the desires of your heart."

Daily Requests

- Ask God to teach our families to trust Him and do good.

- Pray that God will bring people to great hope with a saving knowledge of the Lord Jesus Christ.

- Pray that God will restore hope in this nation and cause godly principles to be followed for His glory and for our future.

Lord, we ask You to teach our families to trust You and do good. Give us your sight and vision in our lives.

Fifteen Years

"I will add fifteen years to your life. And I will deliver you and this city from the hand of the king of Assyria. I will defend this city for my sake and for the sake of my servant David" (2 Kings 20:6).

Hezekiah had become ill and was at the point of death. The prophet Isaiah told him that the Lord said he would not recover, but Hezekiah turned his face to the wall and prayed to the Lord. God answered through His prophet Isaiah and told Hezekiah He would heal him.

God did not only answer his prayer for healing, though. God also promised that He would not only bring healing but also deliver him and the city from their enemy. Does God answer prayer? He answers, and sometimes we get more than we ask for—and He loves to do it.

What is it today that you need and your family needs from God? Ask for it. Walk in His ways and follow Him always, for He is faithful.

Daily Requests

- Ask God for what you need.

- Pray that He will place compassion into the heart of His people for those who do not know Him.

- Pray that God will cause godly people and principles to rise up in this nation and make a difference for Christ.

Lord, I ask You to instill compassion for the lost into the hearts of Your people. May we love others with Your love.

Bibliography

Randy Krehbiel World Staff Writer. "Tarnished Gold." Tulsa World, June 16, 2007, Copyright 2011. World Publishing Co.

LIVE

listen|imagine|view|experience

AUDIO BOOK DOWNLOAD INCLUDED WITH THIS BOOK!

In your hands you hold a complete digital entertainment package. In addition to the paper version, you receive a free download of the audio version of this book. Simply use the code listed below when visiting our website. Once downloaded to your computer, you can listen to the book through your computer's speakers, burn it to an audio CD or save the file to your portable music device (such as Apple's popular iPod) and listen on the go!

How to get your free audio book digital download:

1. Visit www.tatepublishing.com and click on the elLIVE logo on the home page.
2. Enter the following coupon code:
   8b5d-097c-1116-4878-c842-c753-8839-0b8c
3. Download the audio book from your elLIVE digital locker and begin enjoying your new digital enter-tainment package today!